Relationship Split

A helping hand towards
your recovery from a
relationship breakdown

Martin J. Whelan

iUniverse, Inc.
New York   Bloomington

Relationship Split
A helping hand towards your recovery
from a relationship breakdown

iUniverse books may be ordered through booksellers or by contacting:

iUniverse
1663 Liberty Drive
Bloomington, IN 47403
www.iuniverse.com
1-800-Authors (1-800-288-4677)

Because of the dynamic nature of the Internet, any Web addresses or links contained in this book may have changed since publication and may no longer be valid.

ISBN: 978-1-4401-8131-3 (sc)
ISBN: 978-1-4401-8130-6 (ebk)

Printed in the United States of America

iUniverse rev. date: 12/17/2009

Contents

Foreword

As you are reading this my guess would be that you are feeling raw from your relationship split. You want answers. You want guidance. You want to find your way out of the hole you are in, and fast!

I can say these things because I have been there. I have experienced the emotions you are going through. I have arrived at that point where I knew this was not a dress rehearsal or a dream; it was in fact for real. I have felt the shock of separation.

I understand the pain you are experiencing. The tiredness, the anxiety, the queasiness you feel inside your stomach. The seeming loss of control of where you thought your life was heading.

For the first two months after my relationship split I was a complete mess. Unable to work, experiencing massive mood swings from constant tears to raging anger whilst continually turning the situation over in my mind. Searching for answers, searching for comfort, but always I would end up in the same place as I had started. What could I do?

In my working life involving both corporate and private clients, I utilise the practices of Neuro Linguistic programming, Modern Psychology, Eastern Philosophy and Quantum Physics. This breadth of awareness and comprehension enabled me amongst other things to help transform businesses losing millions of pounds per year back into a profitable position, lead a company to double sales turnover within a 12 month period, stop individuals from self destruction by changing their perspectives on how they see the world and provided to others an array of different understandings that literally changed the course of their lives.

Now I was the one in need of assistance. After this 2 months, which I can only describe as mourning, I began to realise that I had at my disposal a vast bank of research, analysis and, most importantly, practical experience in the area of emotional intelligence, from which I could draw knowledge, direction and specific actions. However, rather than applying this information to others I now had to see whether I could use these gifts for myself. Could I really turn my life around from what at that time looked a complete disaster?

Well, I am still here to tell the tale and I have written this book to share with you these incredible understandings and philosophies, together with the recovery strategies I created and utilised myself. I have written in straightforward vocabulary without any jargon to provide the tools and methodologies within a format you can immediately put into action.

You do not need to know, for example, the theory of Neuro Linguistic Programming to use the benefits it gives. I have provided a brief introduction into each of the practices I use in the back of the book, and I encourage you to investigate the subjects for yourself if you so choose.

As a template, and to encourage you to comprehensively take stock of your current position, I have used my personal story as the spine of the book. Whilst describing parts of my childhood, my married and my working life, I also highlight the major challenges encountered along the way and how they subsequently impacted upon our relationship. I reveal how my limiting beliefs were dramatically affecting the quality of my life and I demonstrate how we can transform the way we see and feel about ourselves to fully enjoy each day and opportunity.

Step 1 in each chapter outlines the subject we are looking to explore. Step 2 brings the subject to life using my personal story for substance and examples. Step 3 asks you to complete an exercise related to the subject using your personal experience. Step 4 provides you with detail on the practice we have used for the exercise. You will discover that each subject, once explored and acted upon, becomes a piece of your path towards your recovery.

I have not created this book to illustrate how to attract your next partner, although, strangely enough, by taking the actions described you will naturally become more attractive than ever before, a brilliant incentive in its own right I am sure you would agree.

I have created this book to enable you to rediscover yourself. To help you know who you are as an individual. To learn how you tick. To understand how you see your world and enable you to uncover the real issues you need to face in order to enhance your speed of recovery from your relationship split.

Once you truly know who you are you are ready to go back into the relationship marketplace; however you will be going there as a very different person. You will be a person who is in control. You will be a person who knows what they want and where they are heading. You will be a person who has looked at themselves from the inside out and re-discovered their own true personality and worth. Fundamentally, you will be a person who is not afraid to open your arms and let another into your life. You will operate with a new found level of trust and you will have a massive desire to fully explore and rejoice in your new relationship.

Introduction

In today's world there seems to be an epidemic of relationships that fail or breakdown, leaving behind them a trail of hurt, sorrow, anger, heartache, loneliness, emptiness, despair (recognise any of these?).

After many years of studying the human psychology, I know that everyone's experience will be different dependant upon their life's events to date. We all have 'our story', a framework and tapestry of how we have come to be where we are today. No two people will see or feel exactly the same about a situation or event that occurs. It entirely depends upon your interpretation according to your values, beliefs and experiences to this point.

When a relationship breaks down I feel there is a distinct difference between whether you are, in my phraseology, the 'receiver' or the 'initiator' of the split. I was the receiver of the news "I no longer love you the way I did", and with this my main feeling was a total loss of control over the situation.

My mind was in turmoil for weeks, if not months. Did I see the split coming? I believe I did. Did I want to see it coming? No. I thought we could resolve every difficulty through debate, analysis of the facts and agreeing a solution to the issue (does this sound like the man?). However the core of the relationship was missing, that indefinable feeling inside that had created the bond between us, a bond that had lasted 30 years.

In the course of describing my experiences, I hope to stimulate thoughts and feelings about your own personal relationship history. I want you to reflect on how the 'events' you have experienced have led you to your current position.

I would like you to face your fears with me. From talking to many people on the subject of a relationship breakdown, it is clear that a reaction that frequently occurs is the 'Fight or Flight' syndrome. This reaction causes us to consider whether we should attack or run away from the reality of our situation. We may try to cover things up using work, fitness, alcohol, solicitors, anti depressants, illegal drugs or sex as deflections from our issues. We may consider moving away in order to escape, to run away from this painful situation however the central issues, the core issues, still remain, issues that fundamentally shape our relationship lives.

To further enable you to move forward, I want you to confront a number of other key areas. For instance, how are you interpreting the position you find yourself in today? What feelings, such as loneliness, are traumatising you at this time? How is your ego affecting the way you are handling your situation? What 'rules' have you created, consciously or subconsciously, that may be dramatically curtailing your ability to move on? How much blame and anger are you feeling towards your previous partner? How, considering all that has happened, can you start to trust again?

I believe that my 'event' happened to give me the opportunity to tackle my issues, should I be brave enough to face them. I could try until my dying days to work out what went wrong and to blame my wife for everything, but I knew, deep down, that the only thing I could truly change in this world was me.

I could use this experience to go backwards and become a victim of the situation, or I could take this opportunity with both hands, arms, feet, legs, head and torso and find again the person I was before life's events took their toll.

Through my personal reflections and actions I discovered how much of the cause of our marriage failure was due to my view of the world and the issues I had. My wife too had her own issues that affected us, but rather than concentrate on these I decided to work on the only person I was totally in charge of - myself.

We are in this world for such a relatively short space of time when matched against the overall scheme of existence. I believe that we should give ourselves the opportunity to live a fantastic life rather than be paralysed, or at best limited in our growth, because of an event that occurs or a relationship that ends.

A number of years before my relationship split happened I attended a seminar by an American Motivational Speaker, Anthony Robbins. In the aspect of relationship difficulties he suggested a healing method for moving on could simply be to alter what we say to ourselves. The changing of our inner dialogue from "Why did this person leave me?" to "Thank God they left so they can make room for someone who is right for me" could help transform our progress. His challenge was very direct, very strong, but is he not right?

Changing fundamental aspects of your long held beliefs and views on life takes time and perseverance. I have not tried here to create a quick fix, a 'sticking plaster' approach for your recovery. If you are prepared to really look at yourself in order to move forward there will be work involved. There will be a necessity to look at who you are from a different perspective, perhaps for the first time

Before you read any further please get a journal, a note book or pad. I would like you to do the exercises as you read so that you are totally in tune with the essence of the issue we are dealing with.

Thank you for allowing me to share these insights and strategies with you. I want to give hope to everyone who is dealing with the huge effects of a relationship split that, with the right mindset, friends, belief and love, the emotional turmoil you currently feel can be turned into a fantastic future, your anger can be turned to joy, you will again wake up looking forward to the day and you can use your life's experiences to grow as the special person you are.

The Journey Begins

When we understand the reasons why people are so different we can begin to comprehend why conflict and misunderstandings are so prevalent in our relationships.

Our brain stores every event that we experience throughout our lifetime. This fact begins to explain how our personality and individual characteristics form and why to some people a spider is a beautiful creature, of historical significance and integral to the evolution of the planet, and to others it is the most fearful monster that must be killed at all costs; 'immediately'.

From the day that we are released into the world we are being moulded into the shape of things to come. Social backgrounds, family dynamics, environment, finances and geography are a few of the elements that quickly start to shape our perspectives on life and, in particular, the way we view the world.

Our starting points can be very different. Some people can come from a background of immense wealth, privilege, and quantifiable 'things', yet lack any true feeling of being part of a compassionate loving family. Another person may on the surface lack everything materialistic but they have a foundation, an inner strength, gained as the result of a warm, comforting and caring upbringing. These nurturing elements support that person throughout their entire life, enabling them to give these basic but crucial needs to others as it is part of what they are, part of what they have always experienced, it is in fact their normal way of being.

We are the most complicated creatures on earth. We are capable of many wondrous things; vaccines for illnesses that would previously have wiped out generations of the populous, flight to other planets, instantaneous communication using the airwaves, information technology, even the replacement of vital organs within the body.

Yet the human being is also a complete contradiction. Our ability to think and use conscious thought and reasoning stands us apart from the rest of the animal kingdom. But this is where the dichotomy begins. Because of the uncontrolled use of conscious thought, where we continually strive to seek resolutions to problems, both real and perceived, we can create for ourselves a mass of emotional and mental disturbance in our everyday lives.

I would like you to start this journey armed with some very basic statements that may help release you from your current level and type of thinking:

- Every human being on the planet is different
- If everyone were the same what a boring world this would be
- No two people will see the same event in exactly the same way
- What you see, feel, hear and believe is your own truth and not the truth of anyone else
- The only person you can take full responsibility for is you
- By taking responsibility to control the type and quality of thoughts you have in your mind you can

dramatically change the way in which your life will evolve

- You can choose the way you live. You can shield yourself from the possibility of further hurt from relationships or you can experience the rush of emotions when you first meet, taste the beauty of closeness, feel your heart race when you hear them on the phone, delight in seeing someone flower before you or feel great just by simply holding their hand. The choice is yours.

Exercise 1 - Gratitude

Although you may find this exercise tough to begin with, it is a brilliant way to change how you are feeling. After my relationship split, I really struggled to perform this exercise as my overwhelming thoughts were of the bad things that had occurred and the position I found myself in. However, as I used this exercise constantly throughout the days, weeks and months that followed, I started to see that there were indeed things that were great in my life. My son, my mother and father, my dog, my friends; I even had food to eat as the supermarket had delivered the shopping to my back door!

Use this exercise daily. Think of new things to feel grateful for; nature, your health, a phone call just when you needed it, that smile you received from a complete stranger. These may sound basic, simple, but are they not part of the core of life?

- *What are you grateful for in your life right now?*
- *List all of the great things that have happened to you in your life so far. The holidays, the day you met a special friend, your schooldays, parties, finding that brilliant self help book, a prize you won, walking in*

> the pouring rain,   days when it felt brilliant just being
> you.

- *Who do you have around you now?*
- *Detail all of the people who care for you.*

The practice of gratitude is designed to change your mental state, releasing you from a negative or sorrowful position. As a key practice of Quantum Physics and Buddhism, gratitude helps us to remember what is good about our lives today, what we have around us now and how fortunate we are. This practice moves us also into the here and now, subsequently elevating the quality of our thinking.

The Forming of a Relationship

Is it luck or is it fate? When two people meet all kinds of dynamics are released. Who are they really behind what you first see? How does a chance meeting turn into a long term relationship?

My wife and I met in 1976 when she was still 15, at a disco hosted by the then local hero DJ Stevie Dee. My wife was my kind of girl, very slim (I had no idea she was recovering from anorexia), had black hair in the bob cut which I loved, black jeans, floral patterned platform shoes, a thin neck scarf and a t-shirt with imitation braces with fists in the appropriate places; and I still married her!

The other recollection of that night was my own attire. I had just passed my 17th birthday and my presents had included a patterned polo shirt and wide beige flares that of course, in 1976, went over the top of high platform shoes and reached the floor.

The disco was in a local village hall and drinks were served from behind a table in the corner. During the course of the evening the floor gradually became wet due to the drink being spilt and the high humidity generated by the sheer volume of teenagers packed into this small hall. The combined liquid then started to soak up my trousers, reaching my knees by the end of the evening, an ensemble which created a majestic two tone effect! And she still married me!

We lived 10 miles apart, which required travelling either by bus, by parent in my wife's case, or by my father bringing me as part of a driving lesson. As mentioned, these were the days of the platform shoe (for once I felt tall, but everyone was wearing them so it really made no difference) and my father would not let me wear them to drive. Now I don't regard it as cool to reach the meeting point with your beloved and then have to change your shoes in front of her, but she didn't seem to mind, perhaps it was just my ego calling!

As with many relationships that start this early we went through the usual together - break up - together phase, which of course led to the phone calls that lasted for hours! It is amazing to recount that we would be together for the evening and then be on the phone when we got home, either to sort out the argument we had just had or just to talk some more. At this time in my home we had a 'party line' with another resident in the maisonettes where I lived; they must have been totally fed up with me and my hours of incessant talking to my future wife.

On leaving school at 16 I joined a local business as an apprentice engineer. The rate of pay was very poor, in fact I used to earn more working after school and on a Saturday at the local ironmongers, but in retrospect this grounding has stood me in great stead over the years. I was never happy being an engineer, a common theme as you will see, and continually dreamed and talked to my future wife about owning a garage or some type of business in the future.

My wife was still at the High School for Girls in the 5th year. She was far more academic than me, gaining 8 O' Levels, but she always felt that she had to work really hard to gain her rewards as opposed to her younger brother who had, and still has, a great brain for memory and recall.

My wife's family were very interesting in makeup. I got on really well with her father, who was a salesman for a German medical company. He too had the same trait as my wife where he worked extremely hard for his position, and I admired him for this. On reflection, I wonder, with those of us who do not consider ourselves 'naturally gifted at what we do', and who continually feel that we have to work harder for our rewards, whether we truly realise the potential long term damage that can be caused to ourselves and those around us?

As I had a poor relationship with my father until much later in life my wife's father became an important figure to me. He treated me very well and I was interested in what he did, especially as selling had started to appeal to me as it encompassed a company car, nice clothes, better rewards and not having to clean the ring of grease from the bath every night!

There was no doubt that my wife was the apple of his eye. They were similar in nature, being quite quiet but with a gregarious strain that came out every so often. They did not like arguments as they could become emotional very quickly; not aggressive or striking out, but quite often failing to get their point across before the tears would form.

My wife's mother was different as she had very strong opinions and would voice them eloquently and forcefully. Her two sons have the same characteristics. She did not talk about herself that much and, I believe, this is something my wife shared with her. My wife would keep herself to herself and not communicate what she was thinking until it came out emotionally (as I was to find out along the way and especially 30 years later).

My wife, as previously recalled, had suffered from anorexia during her early teenage years and this had a major impact upon the family. Seeing someone you love inflicting this level of pain on themselves must have been harrowing and this later surfaced with deep feelings voiced by her brother as to how this impacted on his life during these early years.

At this time in the mid-70s anorexia was not well recognised as it is today. My wife had real issues with the psychologists she saw at the time who tried to disgrace her into 'pulling herself together' continually asking her "Can't you see what you are doing to your family?" It was fortunate that my wife's parents were resourceful and continued to seek help from different sources.

When I recall asking my wife why she decided to start eating again she said; "One day I saw the look of despair on my mother's face and I did not want to see it anymore".

She then started on the road to recovery and I had no idea at the time we met that I was to become an integral part of this. I just remember seeing that young lady in the disco who was 'my kind of girl'.

Exercise 2 - Recognise, Not Deny

This exercise is designed to make you recognise some of the key elements of why you fell in love with this person and how it starts to formulate your history. Never try to deny what was good, instead use this for your future references. Doesn't this seem a better way of looking at things, as opposed to thinking about what you might have lost? You still have it all inside! That is why it goes through your mind all of the time but you keep trying to push it away. I want you to allow your thoughts rather than to deny them. This is the only way to long term recovery and happiness, I assure you.

I can see many of you now boiling with the thought that "I can't think of anything good about 'that' person at this time". However, I would like to encourage you to open this perhaps painful door.

Look back at the early part of your relationship and journal your thoughts and recollections:

- *How did you meet*
- *What do you remember about when you first met*
- *What was it about them that appealed to you*
- *What made them different from others you might have dated*

The suppression of our feelings and emotions are incredibly damaging to our physical and relational health. Eastern philosophy encourages us to keep a balanced perspective on events that occur to us. Revealing the positive aspects of your relationship demonstrates why you were attracted to this person and why you enjoyed being with them. Do not deny what was good. Use this sustenance for your next relationship as you have now revealed a number of things you look for in your partner.

As a Child

Our start in life sets the scene for many years to come. Many of us spend a huge amount of time and energy dealing with our initial view of the world.

My own family life was quite difficult. My parents come from two large Irish families, but in the main this is where the similarities end. My mother's family are exactly how you would imagine a large family to be: very tight knit, supportive and caring. My Grandmother, of whom you will hear more throughout this book, the only grandparent I have known, was an extraordinary character, having brought up a family of 13 from a young age when my grandfather died early.

I am sure that behind the scenes there was and is conflict, as the story of this particular family is worthy of a book in itself. For the purposes of this scene setting, however, nurture and support is a key feature of the family trait.

My father's family on the other hand were quite different, as they appeared to have been emotionally damaged from a young age. They lost both of their parents early and essentially had to bring themselves up, a situation I find difficult to comprehend. Unfortunately this early experience left deep scarring with most of the brothers who I knew, and this in turn translated into their relationships.

I have never had a close relationship with my father, interestingly, until now. He was always critical of anything I said and rose to great anger very quickly if he thought he had been spoken back to or that I disagreed with his point of view.

This left me with deep scars which took me many years to start to repair. They say that it can take you 40 years to get over the first 7, and I really believe this to be the case.

Every one of us is different. We react to stimulus with different responses and with subsequent outcomes. I started at an early age to have difficulties with anyone who was stern or shouted at me. I would do my utmost not to expose myself to the possibilities of being wrong. This method of handling my situation became totally self defeating. I always felt pressure to be prepared to prove my point. I tried to second guess any situation that might occur in order again to be prepared. I had an unconscious feeling that everyone was going to criticise me. All in all, this coping strategy put tremendous strain on me. It provoked massive stress and completely sapped my energy. I believe I functioned (being the operative word) like this until I reached 40 when, through another set of circumstances, I made the decision to tackle the way I had been living my life up until this point in time.

> # Exercise 3 - Define / Determine / Discard

People in psychology call this exercise many things; for our purpose we will call it 'Gunny Sacking'.

'Gunny Sacking' can best be described as listing all of the 'events' 'issues' or 'complications' that we carry around with us, quite often negative in nature. These events shape our characters and can create major blocks to our progress as adults.

Just think, how would it feel to be able to pick up all of the negative memories and change them?

After doing this exercise you have the power to decide to let these limiting memories go! You can use this opportunity for your personal gain and then, if they serve no future purpose, dispose of them! The past has happened, why live back there? Discard what you do not need and move on.

- *Look into your life so far. List down some of the significant impacts you might have experienced, both really great and those that were not so.*
- *Split the list into two, one being positive events and the other being negative (I bet the negatives are easier to remember, aren't they?!)*
- *Look now at the experience that the event brought you. Determine what you can learn from it? Remember to try and identify the positive aspects as well as the negative*
- *Why do you think it happened, and, possibly, did you have something to do with its manifestation?*
- *How could you use this learning to better yourself in the future?*
- *Can you now change the way you view this potentially limiting episode to your benefit?*
- *Now that you have examined and taken the useful part of this memory I want you to feel, hear and imagine yourself throwing it into the dustbin, placing it on the bonfire, dropping it into the ocean or any such vision that enables you to discard this unwanted aspect of your history.*

One of the most powerful tools utilised in Neuro Linguistic Programming is the practice of Reframing. By examining the current 'framework', or the meaning that we currently apply to an event that has happened to us, we can create a new, more beneficial meaning that will support us rather than hinder. Time will have elapsed since the event and by using a wider perspective you may now be able to see potential benefits from the situation that would not have been apparent at the time the event occurred.

The Journey
Continues

There are many different philosophies that exist in the world related to the journeys that our lives take. Do we self determine? Are we at the mercy of circumstance? Are we in full control of our destiny? Do we have no control of our destiny? Are we being guided along a path by an invisible hand? A complex subject but the basics are simple; we are where we are.

We cannot go back, we cannot un-wrap our experiences to date and mould them into something new - or can we? By allowing ourselves the opportunity to acquire a fresh interpretation of our past experiences, by deciding to take the right action for our situation today, we can pave the way towards a healthy mind and perspective on life.

I had a deep set belief that my working life was always going to be hard due to my seeming lack of education and, I have to say, my disinterest in formal education. I suppose I just didn't get it, learning things by rote just so that you knew your times tables, but what was the practical application of them, why have a letter instead of a number rather than the number itself? I lost interest totally at the start of secondary school, not because I had a higher purpose but because I just didn't see the relevance. Each school day was something to get through rather than to get something from. I am not saying I am right in this matter, I now study continuously, but this was how it was for me at that time.

I started my working life whilst still at school with the proverbial paper round, a vocation which proved to be a fantastic learning opportunity on how to outfox and outrun the local stray dogs of the area. My next adventure was working in a hardware shop after school and all day Saturday. The owner of the shop was a great, chain smoking lady called Mrs Smith (never knew her first name) with a slobbering boxer dog who was always in close proximity to keep me on my toes. We sold all the traditional hardware items, nails, screws, door bolts, sink plugs, chain, plus a variety of lamps and glass vases. I am sure my mother soon became quite sick each birthday and Christmas when she would receive yet another highly coloured glass vase to adorn her sideboard.

One particular duty that was challenging, especially in winter, was the selling of paraffin for the indoor heaters of the time. Amazing to think now, but at that time we had a tank in an outdoor building of the shop from which we would take the required gallon and put it into any type of container the customer had. I also distinctly remember that just one drop of paraffin spilt on your hand and you would own that odorous musk the whole day; I can still smell it now.

I loved being with the people in the shop and felt that I treated them well, but I had real issue; I couldn't remember where things were. Mrs Smith quite often told me I was "bloody useless", but she still kept me on; I suppose my 'people' side was starting to come out at this stage, and she could see that although I might take 10 minutes to find something the customers were generally ok with me.

Today we expect our children to define their careers from an early age, developing an educational strategy to enable them to get there, usually via O' Levels (now GCSE's), A' Levels and University, with the result that they end up in a place which they could visualise years before.

How many of us, if we are truly honest, know what we will be doing tomorrow, let alone in 3, 5 or 10 years time? I believe for the majority of people we follow a path that appears to be the right thing to do on the surface, reacting to what others say we should do or be, but inside, could there be a wanderer lurking? For many years I fought this wanderer person inside of me, I did not recognise that this was just me, that I needed fresh stimulus on a regular basis. Inside I knew I could not contemplate doing the same thing for 30 years, but when I compared myself to others, who had performed the same role for many years; I thought "What is wrong with me. Why can't I settle down and be content doing the same job?" I understand this part of my character now, but it took me a great deal of time to work it out!

My first full time job was an Apprentice Engineer with a forklift truck company 100 yards from my back door. I remember going to the interview with their Personnel Manager, who was very smart in a pin striped suit of the day and gleaming black shoes. I turned up wearing a denim jacket with a badge that promoted the much ahead of its time value to 'Save Water, Shower with a Friend' with intertwined feet depicted in the centre. I got the job but perhaps not the highest score for my dress sense!

I started on the same day as another apprentice who was the son of one of the established members of the Fabrication Team. This was the first time I really noticed my growing tendency to compare myself to others. He appeared confident, technically able and perhaps a bit cocky. I, on the other hand, felt out of my depth. Again, my lack of memory issue started to emerge where I didn't feel I could remember how to do something, even though I had done it fine, say, a week previously. In my mind the other apprentice seemed to be sailing through, and because of his confidence he was.

Now in a mature state I would have recognised that my lack of confidence and the way I felt about myself were the inhibitors to me moving forward. But then, and for years to come, I looked on these others as the lucky ones; they had not had the issues I had had in my life, they had better starts, had better resources, were cleverer than I, did not have learning issues, were better connected - I could go on for ages.

As I write this I can still feel that whole scenario re-emerge very powerfully. How did it manifest at the time without this mature perspective? My main feelings were of anger, stress, resentment and a distinct lack of energy. These feelings were all held together by negative thoughts that continually raced around my mind in ever non-resolvable circles.

My four year apprenticeship included three years of day release to college. A wide range of apprentices from various companies across the area converged on High Wycombe Technical College each Wednesday for table football practice. It was amazing how we fitted the four lessons into the day, as a testosterone filled group of guys competed at the highest level for supremacy on the table.

The favourite lesson of the day was a General Studies session just after lunch, perfectly timed I am sure, which captivated us and was led by an excellent tutor who shared with us his passion for history surrounding the Roman games. His seeming speciality appeared to focus on the more erotic and sexually terrifying feats that poor maidens were subjected to in the course of 'entertainment'. Sometimes I wonder how far we have moved on from these times, perhaps not far, but that is another topic!

Towards the end of our apprenticeships my colleague and I had started going out to the customers' premises to repair and maintain their trucks. At first we accompanied more experienced engineers, and then we received service vans, becoming fully fledged Field Service Engineers.

Again, from a technical perspective I never felt fully competent, but in most cases I really enjoyed the interface with the customers, solving problems, making sure that both the managers and the drivers were ok with what was happening.

However there was a distinct issue; I hated getting dirty every day. Each night I would get into the bath and produce a clearly distinguishable tide mark about ¾ of the way up the tub. My hands were continually chapped and cut, oil and grease seemed to ingress into the skin, and I never felt really clean. Add to these issues the fact that I never felt really technically competent, and I had all of the ingredients for yet more dissatisfaction.

Exercise 4 - Self Perception

This exercise is to help you look deeply at yourself to start to examine your core beliefs. You have to be very open with yourself, ignore the calling of your ego which will encourage you to not want to expose these deep seated thoughts. I am here to tell you that within this box of statements your happiness lies. At this moment they may appear like little devils that have continually plagued you but you have continually tried to cover them, quieten their calling. This is the time for you to look them square in the face and really see what they are saying, how they are limiting your future, and to start to enable you to put them into a perspective that will release you towards a fantastic future.

Remember, you are writing in a safe environment, no one else need ever see what you are detailing, this is just for you. Be brave, don't cover anything up, and allow your most core feelings to surface. I hope now you are encouraged to complete this exercise.

- *Look back at your early years, perhaps from 14 to 25, and try to remember how you thought about yourself then. What were the issues going through your mind on a continual basis?*
- *How did they make you feel about yourself?*
- *How many of them are still with you today?*
- *With you new skill of 'Reframing' from the last exercise, which reflections are you going to act upon and what and when are you going to put things into action*

From our earliest days we are being programmed with our beliefs and perspectives on life. These beliefs we take as fact within our everyday living. Through the NLP practice of 'Reframing' you can now determine if these beliefs you have are still correct or relevant. Are they empowering or restricting you as an individual today? Beliefs are hard wired into the workings of the brain. Major effort may be required to alter their power over you; however the rewards to you in time will be dramatic.

Growing Up

As we journey forward, a continuation of events, good and some not so good, will come along to steer the traveller along his destined path.

One part of my life with which I was not dissatisfied occurred on 2nd May 1980, when my wife and I were married. Our parents did us proud, laying on a great day with a major afternoon and evening of entertainment held at our local town hall following the ceremony at the High Church in the centre of town.

A distinct memory from this day was the arrival of one of my aunties: Auntie Kate. For some reason Auntie Kate felt empowered to not confirm beforehand whether she would be attending, which really frustrated my mother. In the end we decided to set up a place for her and her husband and if they came, then fine.

Well, Auntie Kate did attend: and what an entrance. She wore a hat so large that when she walked in front of one of the Town Hall lights it felt like an eclipse. As the proceedings continued it became patently clear that Auntie Kate had no intention of taking off that hat. Whatever you were doing in amongst 150 plus people, perhaps eating your meal, having a dance or chatting in the lobby, you could still see that hat! Auntie Kate was obviously a fan of the hit TV programme of the time Dallas, and a milliner with little conscience had seen an opportunity to offload a piece of 1980s vintage apparel.

A few months previous to our marriage we had bought a maisonette in a town 20 miles from where we had grown up. Many people of our age were moving there as the house prices were considerably lower than where our parents lived, as the location was deemed to be just outside the London commuter belt; oh, how times have changed!

Thus we entered into married life, evolving a network of friends in this new town, setting out upon the journey of living together and for the first time really getting to know each other's ways and needs.

After seven years of working as an engineer I knew I needed to change my career. I had always noticed the salesmen where I worked had what appeared to be a very cushy number, going out to see customers, talking to them, driving nice cars, obviously earning lots of money, and generally doing not a great deal for great rewards! Naivety is a beautiful thing don't you think?

I decided the time was right to see about a job in sales. Our General Manager at the time was a rather distinctive character who had lost an eye in a shooting accident as a child and a glass eye had been fitted in its place. I always had difficulty when speaking to him in remembering which eye was the good one, in order that I could make the correct level of eye contact during our conversation; unfortunately they moved independently and totally confused me.

He always had the aura of someone you did not mess with. You sensed he could make ruthless decisions and that he enjoyed being totally in control of his business. I summoned my courage and asked for an appointment with him. Sitting down, after being instructed to do so, I blurted out my case for becoming his next superstar salesman. I set before him a proposal of how I believed I had all of the right experience, I detailed why my engineering skills would prove massively beneficial and I described how I had the right amount of application and dedication to succeed. His eloquent response has always remained with me, as I am sure the prose of Shakespeare have remained with others; "As long as you have got a hole in your arse you will never be a salesman!"

Little did I know that 20 years later I would replace him running a large business in the North of London, however there was one hell of a journey to travel first.

I concluded from my General Manager's comment that he did not quite believe that I had the requisite skills to become a salesperson. I pondered for some time but then decided, with the great help of my wife, to accept a commission only sales role selling paint to bakeries, kennels and farmers. Boy: was that General Manager right! I didn't have a clue about selling (not sure how this related to my rectum however) but I was determined to give it a go.

I soon realised that my boyhood paper round had indeed been a tremendous training ground for my new requirement to deal with the protective hounds on the farms. I also deduced that farmers were indeed as tight as everyone says, I found that many kennels provide better facilities for the animals than some humans live in, and that the paint I was selling was a rip off at £75 per kilo tin in 1983!

I worked hard at this new role but after 6 months of very little income I moved to a job selling photocopiers. A step up from the paint sales as it at least had a small salary and potentially high commission, but with our first child on the way I decided to move back, this time as a salesman, to the forklift industry, where I re-established myself within an environment that was to be a superb business and training ground for me over the next 20 years.

Exercise 5 - Some People Can Be So Cruel

These first exercises are designed to 'unearth and cleanse' your history to date. You do not have to be your past if you have the mind set and the determination so to choose.

The mind is naturally negative. Scientific studies reveal that the average human being has 50,000 thoughts a day (many women think men have the same thought 50,000 times a day, but who's counting!). Of these 50,000 thoughts up to 75% can be negative in nature. If we then recall that the method we use to build up a new skill or belief is through repetition, doing it over and over again, consider then the effects of replaying that same CD continuously in our minds of what others have said to us in the past! Every time we repeat the thought it becomes stronger, it becomes hard wired into our brains, it becomes part of our belief system. All of this happens naturally, whether we are aware of this phenomenon or not.

- *List down those instances where people have given you a piece of advice or said something to you that has pierced you through the heart. As human beings we find it far easier to remember the negative things that have occurred than those of a more positive nature.*
- *I really want you to think about these negative events. I want you to look at how they are influencing your current thoughts and actions and how they may be affecting your beliefs and possibly your ambitions for the future.*
- *Now, utilising your 'Reframing' skills, review these events and construct them into a scenario that is beneficial and empowering to you.*

> *Eastern philosophy and Quantum physics describes how we are a spirit that has a body, mind and ego in order to experience the world around us. Unfortunately, most of us are dominated by the mind with its perpetual need to be busy and it's referencing of past and future. For excellent mental and physical health we need to be in control of our mind and its quality of thought, as opposed to being at its mercy from negative continual chatter. Imagine, just silence from your mind, how fantastic would this feel?*

Our View of the World

If you have a certain perspective on how the world operates you can look back and see key people, events and circumstances that occur in our lives which, mostly unforeseen at the time, become hugely important to our future. A fundamental belief I have is that we are co-creators of our worlds.

Most of the time, I feel we see life in general as one challenge following another, a little like an obstacle course. We tackle the first hole of crazy golf, eventually getting the ball through a pipe rather than hitting the sides, it goes round a loop, bounces off a peg and then finally finishes in the desired location, putts taken 15. Then we move onto the next challenge which requires us to hit the ball with just the right level of speed up a see saw, down the bank and into a gully towards the hole, par for the hole 4, your score 17! Now the next 16 holes start to feel like a nightmare to be endured, par for the course 76, already you are at 32, where is the fun in this?!

The forklift company I joined in 1983 was a young business, having been established for only one year. It had been started by a number of highly skilled people coming together from other companies within the industry.

Early on I felt myself under pressure, not from the members of the company but from myself. I constantly reflected on why the others were more successful, that I had much to learn and that somehow I didn't quite fit in, another general belief that I carried for many years.

So now, dragging this sack of issues around with me even before I started my day (does this sound familiar to some of us), the energy I could put into doing the job was probably reduced by 30-40%, remember also that I was still learning how to sell.

I can recall the nights I used to return home and discuss things over and over with my wife, normally in terms that I couldn't do it, that others were much better than me, I would get the sack if I didn't start selling more, etc. My wife throughout all of this time was extremely supportive and continued to encourage me and my efforts.

Tucked away in this business was a man who would become a major influence on my future, not just in my working life but from a much wider perspective. It is interesting to note however that, at this particular time, we had very little to do with each other. He was on the service side, I was in sales, he kept his head down and just got on with his job.

My main friend from this time was my Sales Manager, Bob. He continually supported me throughout this period of my career. I know at this time I had a huge negative belief system in operation. I would endeavour to deflect any criticism of the sales performance by placing blame anywhere but at my door, that it was always 'someone else's issue' not mine. It was service problems, parts support, the high price of the product, the marketplace, the customers, everything that was not under my influence or control.

It is amazing now to reflect on how my mind operated at this time as I come across it again and again in my current coaching life, people feel that they have no control over either their personal or working lives, thus becoming a victim of circumstance.

When we live life unconsciously, when we don't have any direction or plan of where we want to go, when we believe that we do not have any control over our lives, we 'unconsciously' cause events to just 'happen' to us. Unknowingly, we become the victim of circumstance, just rolling from one 'body blow' to the next.

Our unconscious mode of operating collates all of these 'body blow' experiences and bundles them together. As an example, when we are building a bonfire we collect various pieces of flammable materials such as wood, paper, cardboard, cases and furniture. Once assembled, we bundle them together, set them alight and a major fire is created. These collective elements have a raging heat and intensity, the fire is long lasting and overwhelmingly powerful.

Alternatively, I want you to imagine that each element is lit individually. How have the dynamics of the situation changed? The heat is far less intense as the separated element burns only as an individual item. The time the fire lasts is dramatically reduced, the maintenance of the ashes takes far less tending, in essence, each element is far easier to manage. This 'breaking down' of the elements (or events) provides us with the opportunity to be more in control of the situation. We are able to see far more clearly what is happening and it enables us to deal more easily with the consequences.

My challenge to you here is this; can you now start to see that life might work in a very different way to how you previously perceived? Can you begin to embrace that there is an overriding plan for you in which you can consciously take part and create the future you desire? Rather than see your life as just a number of challenges that merge into one, you can look for a meaning behind each event that has happened to you, gain from understanding this meaning and then move on!

The way in which we interpret events will, I believe, provide us with our futures. We can use our memories to review what the intention was behind any event and hopefully see a different purpose or reason than the one we originally gave it, especially if it is more useful to us for our future lives. Look at these events individually rather than bundle them together. As opposed to trying to move forward through the mire of compounded events see and feel the true meaning of each separate piece of learning.

Exercise 6 - Lessons from History

Later on we will look at a principle called 'fight or flight' but at this stage I would like you to reflect upon whether your current actions and activities are working for or against you. In the early stages of a relationship split there is a tendency to keep busy, to keep yourself distracted and to reduce your time to think to a minimum.

I know from my own experience that this strategy works for a while but there came a point where exhaustion and fatigue overwhelmed me. This left me with no alternative other than to review all of the actions I had undertaken. I needed to establish which actions would help to move me forward and which ones I had been using to camouflage my situation.

This exercise is in 2 parts. Part 1 asks you to reflect again on what has occurred to you in order to find another meaning that may now be more beneficial to you. I want you to 'cleanse your cupboards' to enable you to move forward quickly.

Part 2 asks you to review the current issues you are dealing with and determine whether you can directly influence the issue, are you dependant on others to do something related to the issue, is there nothing you can do about it, or is your involvement in this issue a further complication in your life at this present time?

For instance, giving up smoking is directly influenced by you and you are fully empowered to start the process of giving up. You would immediately benefit financially from this action, which may be extremely important at this moment in time, plus you will feel good about yourself for taking a positive step. You might need to get assistance from your doctor or health clinic but you can take this action without any restrictions to making it happen.

In another example, you may feel very passionately about a military conflict somewhere in the world and you would like to become a campaigner, or help with fundraising. However if your main issue at present is earning enough money to ensure you have shelter and food, then the military conflict, although one you may be passionate about, should move into being a further complication in your life at this time. You recognise that in your current position you cannot directly influence the outcome so it is best to leave it to others and to use your energy elsewhere.

These further complication areas can also turn into a trap. We can start to deny the reality of things 'in our own house', push important things away to do later, involve ourselves in 'other distracting activities' rather than dealing with our own central issues.

> This perspective may seem harsh. I would challenge however that the higher cause is to ensure your own house is in order first and then you can return refreshed and re-energised at a later stage to these other issues if you so choose.

Part 1

- *List out the significant events that have happened in your lifetime, both the positive ones and the negative, or those you perceive as negative.*
- *What lessons can you take from these? Really drill down into the item. Look for the opportunity to interpret it in a different way that feels more empowering.*
- *How do you believe these events have shaped you now as a person?*
- *Is that person the one you want to be?*
- *What do you perceive you would need to change in order to be the person you wish to be or return to being?*

Part 2

- *I would like you to take from your last list what you feel are your Key issues at this point in your life. You can also add other issues that you believe you have or are involved with; for example: not enough friends, not enough money, finding a new partner, wanting to lose or gain weight, giving up smoking or chocolate, the state of the economy, a war in a certain place in the world.*
- *At the end of each issue identify whether you can directly influence this situation, or whether the issue is something that is a further complication in your life at this present time. Come back to your list at a later date once your most urgent are concluded.*

The main benefit we can take from our past experience is the learning it provides. The Buddhist practice of evaluation is a powerful tool for dealing with the impact of any situation. Are you able to do anything about what has happened? Yes. Do what you are able to do. You are in control. Are you able to do anything about what has happened? No. Determine that you cannot take any action. You are still in control as you have made this decision. Do not try to alter things with your mind by pondering 'what if's' or 'if only'. The facts are before you, act only on these.

Gary

"You never know what's around the corner" a phrase that can be translated in so many ways. Do we flow with life or resist it? Can we find the pieces of gold amongst the rocks that stand in our way?

In 1984 our first son Gary was born. I believe it is true that if you really planned on a piece of paper whether you could afford a child you would never do it but my wife gave me the confidence that we could make it work and I am so pleased that she proved to be correct.

Gary was born on 8th September 1984, weighing in at 7lb 5oz, which was an average weight for babies at the time. Thinking of the birth, a significant memory comes back to me that I would like to highlight to all people who are assisting in the delivery of the new born. Please ensure that you remove your rings from your hands. The squeezing of my hand by my wife, who was all of 8 stone wringing wet, resulted in the imprint of a signet ring being visible for months in the third finger of my right hand! Oh how I suffered!

We soon discovered that our son had a very healthy pair of lungs and let the world know that he was really pleased to be free to taste the world from the outside. We also discovered something else. The doctors informed us that he had *Congenital Talipese Equino Varus,* or a condition more commonly known as 'Club Feet'. This is a defect at the ankles where the muscles and ligaments have not formed correctly and can affect 1 in 1000 babies within the UK. The insteps of his feet were pointing inward towards the other leg as opposed to a normal straight down position.

Suddenly all of your plans change. The birth of a child is a fantastic natural event. You have planned how you will dress them, decorated the bedroom, purchased the cot and hedged your bets on the colours of the baby-grows to cater for both sexes. Suddenly you are told that your new baby has a problem and that an appointment has been made at the orthopaedic hospital to see a specialist!

A few days after the birth we arrived at the orthopaedic hospital for our first consultation. We met an extraordinary doctor and man, called Mr Benson who I believe is a magician in his chosen art form. His empathy with us as very nervous young parents, his care of our son whilst he examined him, the natural aura of his personality all created an atmosphere of hope and confidence.

Mr Benson told us that Gary's degree of Talipese was quite severe. Although he fully expected him to walk, he informed us that we should not expect him to become an athlete as, like all sufferers of this condition, his calf muscles would not form to any great extent. I had always played football, and of course wanted this opportunity for my son, but when faced with the prospect of him not being able to walk versus his not having the ability to play competitive sports, this desire of mine paled into insignificance. We had to tackle this situation as it was presented to us rather than think about what we had previously wanted or had perceived the future to be.

Mr Benson also informed us that the initial strategy for Gary would require him to be in plaster for six months, in order to start the process of straightening his feet. The plaster would need to be changed weekly as he grew, and we would have to attend the hospital to have it re-set. Following this initial period he would more than likely require surgery.

We then started a regular routine of hospital appointments. The morning of the visit was filled with removing the plaster to enable our son to have some free time from his casts and to make the appointment quicker. To enact the removal of the casts we used vinegar, as advised, to soften the plaster and then removed the bandages. It is amazing how you adapt to situations when you need to and the process became part of the weekly ritual.

After his six months in plaster it was clear that Gary would indeed require an operation to assist with the straightening. Thinking about such a small bundle as Gary going under a general anaesthetic was extremely nerve wracking and the time from start to finish of the operation seemed an eternity. To our great relief Gary emerged from the operation in great shape and the first of three re-constructive operations had gone very well.

I always find it amazing how you adapt to situations. Six months previously we had been in full anticipation of our new arrival, going about our lives like everyone else, just treating the situation as the norm. Now we were in the midst of continual visits to hospitals, feeling the stress of seeing our small son on a trolley being wheeled to an operating theatre and then experiencing the feeling of relief of his return.

Other facets of the time, however, I remember with a degree of lightness. After the operation Gary had to wear special boots with a brace between them to hold his feet in a horizontal position. This brace became extremely useful in the art of nappy changing! You could hold his legs up by the brace, remove and replace the nappy whilst aided by a very useful piece of apparatus.

Gary also found his uses for the boots and metal brace. They provided him with the ability to stand up at a really young age and enabled him to use the brace on the side of the cot to get our attention. No having to use his throat to gain attention in the mornings for Gary!

And how is Gary now? Just try telling him that he would not be able to play competitive sport. I told you earlier Mr Benson was a magician. Although he is not the fastest around the pitch, Gary has played football for his schools and football clubs from the age of five and he continues to play rugby to a good standard today. Sometimes during his football matches, people would judge Gary as being a slow runner and shout at him to be quicker to the ball or get to a position faster to receive a pass. Although I understood their comments they never realised that just his being there on that pitch was a blessing to us. Whilst I never made the excuse for him, perhaps I should have; if they only knew his journey to be there they might well have thought differently.

I also remember Mr Benson, a leading man in his field in every sense of the word. It was clear that he had dedicated his life to the pursuit of helping people whose lives would be dramatically different without his dedication and expertise. His passion for his art oozed from him with an infectiousness that cascaded into both his patients and his students. He not only changed the lives of the patient but those of the patient's parents and guardians. What a gift to give whilst remaining warm, confident, caring and humble; one of a very special set of people who I have met along the way.

Exercise 7 - Helping Hands

Our aim here is to identify significant people who have influenced our lives and look at the gifts that they have given to us. We are looking for support structures to assist us with a realisation that along our journeys we have met and will continue to meet, special people who are in our lives for the right reasons at the right times. You can call it luck, fate, chance or something predetermined, it is of no real significance. What is of significance is that you look at what these people have given you, the lessons they have taught and use their examples to support yourself along your future path.

One person I think of was my Grandmother. She had an uncanny ability to love everyone, but she also had the gift of being able to make you feel that you were 'just that little more special', never at the expense of comparing you to others but just with the feeling she wrapped you in. I spoke to a cousin of mine about this topic and she said she felt exactly the same when in her presence.

- *List down the influential people you have met along your journey so far. They don't have to be public figures but people who have affected you in a positive, significant way.*
- *What was it about these people that so touched you? What did they do? What did they say? How did they act? What sets them apart from the norm? Make a list.*
- *What specific examples can you take from your list that can significantly assist you with moving forward? Is it their strength, vision, warmth, skill or their love?*

When we choose to view the world in a different way, we see that various people arrive in our lives, at the right time, to help us at that stage of our journey. Many of the philosophies ask us to consider that all of nature is connected. We need to have faith, to take appropriate action and trust that help will be provided when we need it. The key is in the degree of our belief and how we interpret the situations that affect our lives.

The Highs and Lows

Life has a habit of taking you through a myriad of experience to test the resolve of the traveller. These peaks and troughs however can include facing the ultimate challenge.

After 2½ years of struggling to achieve a good result in the young forklift business I had joined, as well as dealing with Gary's needs, my Sales Manager and I had a heart to heart about the situation. He believed that I should consider joining another company that would have the resources to provide me with the formal sales training that I had never had thus giving me the tools to really succeed. Although at first this realisation hurt, in terms of a feeling of failure and starting again, I began to look at my alternatives.

In late 1986 I joined another lift truck business very close to my home. Their philosophy of selling was much more akin to my personality. The sales approach was much more creative, strategic and cost justifiable than the previous method I had employed. I must confess that to begin with I had major difficulties coming to terms with the workload. The sales style called for a great deal of written work, mainly done at night or weekends, resulting in 5½ days working from 7 in the morning till often 9 or 10 at night.

However, little by little the green shoots started to appear and with the greater depth of sales thought and analysis adopted by this business, I started to get results. After struggling for 6 months I found that the tap suddenly started to open up.

Another addition to the family, Paul, came along in September 1987. After the challenges we had had with Gary, we were so relieved that everything appeared normal, and that we could relax into a straightforward lifestyle with success now seeming much more tangible.

In 1988 I became the leading light of the sales operation, breaking records along the way. I was the first salesperson within this business to secure £1m worth of sales from a territory and the first salesperson to achieve 20 deals from new prospects. The principal goals for the sales people were very clear: top salesperson would receive a Mercedes Benz to drive for the following year, and the Sales Director set me a target of a special gift if I achieved 20 new business accounts. Add to these prizes the financial rewards from the truck sales and the bonus scheme, and I was extremely satisfied with what I had obtained from a very successful year.

So there I was, at the top of the tree in my company. We had two fantastic boys, a very secure marriage, Gary was now walking well and improving all the time. There were tangible signs of our success and money in the bank. I had worked extremely hard to achieve this position, been brilliantly supported by my wife, was healthy and had great prospects for the future, what could possible go wrong?

"We are sorry, Mr and Mrs Whelan, but we have found that your son has a disease called 'Glutaric Acidemia' which is a very rare disorder and unfortunately there is no known cure."

Even now as I recall this discussion it is hard to remember that the words were being spoken to my wife and I. Surely this happens to other unfortunate people, not to us. This is something that you see on TV where someone is being told that the one they love will soon not be with them, said to others but not to you.

But this was our reality, staring us in the face. Our son Paul had been ill for six months without a true diagnosis being available. Many trials of different treatments and drugs had been tried, sometimes helping the situation, sometimes making them worse. Our world again had been turned upside down; this time we were facing the ultimate challenge.

Up until 5th May 1989 I had been literally riding a new high. Driving along in my red Mercedes Benz with the shiny emblem at the end of a bonnet that seemed to stretch out forever, I really felt proud of the position we had reached. We moved house, I bought a new car for my wife that mainly sat on the drive, and we booked a nice holiday.

I then received a phone call at work to say that Paul had taken a tumble down a couple of stairs, he seemed ok, but we needed to get him checked out just to be sure.

Glutaric Acidemia Type 1 is a very rare disease which has varying degrees of severity for its sufferers. At the time of Paul's diagnosis there were only three cases known in Europe, and the testing was completed in a facility in Holland. Recent reports highlight that in the United States, with a population of over 300 million people, there are fewer than 100 known cases.

The condition is an organic acid disorder which means that babies cannot remove certain waste products from their blood. The faulty gene only emerges when two carriers have children and pass it to their offspring. For each pregnancy between two carriers there is a 25% chance that the child will be born with the condition. This statistic does not mean, however, that one baby born with the disorder would then result in the following three children being born without. This was a statistic we were to fully understand over the next few years.

Potential Outcome Prognosis from the Medical Journal:

> *This enzyme deficiency disorder is characterized by hypoglycaemia, dystonia (neurologic movement disorder) and dyskinesia (abnormal involuntary movement). After a period of apparently normal development, the disorder may appear suddenly and present as vomiting, metabolic acidosis, hypotonia (decreased muscle tone) and central nervous system degeneration. It is not yet known how or why Glutaric Acid causes brain damage, however damage occurs when a crisis causes an acidic environment in the blood, created by excess protein by-products. Crisis can be provoked by common childhood illnesses such as colds, flu, ear infections, stomach virus, fever etc.*

On 5th May 1989 we were not aware of any of this. All we knew was that Paul had suffered a small fall but had responded to it in an unusual way in that he appeared to have been knocked out and his body went floppy.

Over the next few weeks we spent large amounts of time in hospital and attended consultations, not knowing what was happening to Paul. He had what appeared to be convulsions which made his whole body stiffen and he would sweat profusely.

The initial thoughts were that he was suffering from Cerebral Palsy, which can present in a similar fashion to what we later found out to be the condition known as Glutaric Acidemia. We now started looking at the potential effects of Cerebral Palsy. It appeared that there were varying degrees of the disorder and many children survived well with special help and care. However, after Paul had more motor condition related episodes, the possibility of Cerebral Palsy being the causation behind Paul's illness became more and more unlikely.

After nearly six months of Paul suffering, enduring trials of various drugs and numerous planned and un-planned hospital visits, we had the news we had dreaded. *"We are sorry, Mr and Mrs Whelan, but we have found that your son has a disease called 'Glutaric Acidemia' which is a very rare disorder and unfortunately there is no known cure."*

I had continued to work, from both duty and necessity, throughout a period that now seems a complete daze. I have no real recollection of what happened at work other than getting through the day and mainly visiting Paul and my wife in hospital.

Driving that red Mercedes around and into a hospital car park felt very strange, especially in relation to the high I had felt on receiving the prize and the plaudits only months earlier. But, for future reference, I still had not realised how affected I was by other people's perceptions and the value I placed on what I will call 'external things'. I retained a posture of stiff upper lip, my car could show perhaps the appearance of a doctor I thought, I was always immaculately dressed and rarely let my guard down. In many ways, a very Victorian view on life; don't let anyone see what is happening on the inside!

Gary coped remarkably well during this period. He attended school all of the time and we tried to keep as regular a routine as possible. Friends looked after him after school if my wife or I couldn't get there on time, and our relatives remained close but not intrusive.

During the time with Gary and now with Paul I saw an amazing strength of character in my wife. There was no way that she was not going to cope with this, whatever the situation, and her resolve, substance and depth of energy astounded me. Night after night she would sleep in the hospital on a makeshift bed next to Paul whilst I tried to retain some semblance of normality at home with Gary. I believe that everyone around thought that we had everything under control, and we probably did. However, when you hold this much emotion in check for such sustained periods of time the impact when it is released is dramatic, which I was to find out many years into the future.

Having now received the dreaded news and prognosis a very different perspective began to unfold. How do you accept that your child has a life shortening disease? How do you prepare to configure your life to care for everyone with this knowledge? I am sure we all have thoughts about dying but we always see it as way in the future, it will never happen to me, what will be will be. But now we knew that unless some kind of miracle happened we would have to deal with losing our son, which is not the way it is supposed to happen. The conventional life cycle of dependant to independent, interdependent to dependant would not happen for us here.

I can't recall, as a couple, my wife and I really sitting down and discussing this in depth. As was our way, we dealt with things in a sincere but pragmatic way, doing what had to be done.

During one of our last visits to a mainstream hospital, the medical team suggested that there may be a place available to us at a hospice in Oxford for children with life shortening illnesses, a hospice called Helen House.

Helen House, the first hospice in the world for children, was founded in 1982 by a remarkable woman called Sister Frances Dominica. She had established a friendship with a family whose daughter, Helen, was suffering from a life shortening disease and who required 24-hour care and attention. This sparked within Sister Frances a realisation of a need for a refuge for families to receive respite care for both the ill child and the family as a whole.

Some children came and stayed at Helen House with the carers whilst their parents took a short break. Other families stayed within the hospice close to their child but received much needed rest during the night.

Our first visit to Helen House was extremely daunting. Our perception of a hospice was disinfectant, cold corridors, quiet, sombre decor and most of all unhappiness. We nervously rang the bell and waited for the door to open. To our amazement, rather than being met by a morose, restrained recognition of our plight we were greeted by a level of warmth, care and understanding that quite frankly, I concluded, could not be real. They must be acting. Here were people dealing with one of the most traumatic situations people can face. Here were people totally open, matching what you as individuals needed; a quiet steadying hand, a gentle smile, a listening ear or a huge hug, matched just for you. They appeared to have a common understanding of the human being which is anything but common.

Inside we saw children, some with similar appearances to Paul, others very different, but all with a similar prognosis. Once again we were in the hands of some very special people.

With Paul's diagnosis now confirmed, the correct medication for his condition could now be provided to help control the symptoms. He could no longer eat food, so all of his sustenance had to be via a special fluid diet introduced, as were the drugs, through a tube passing through his nose into the stomach. The tube was kept in place by a plaster on his cheek which I can distinctly remember having to be tenderly looked after otherwise a sore would quickly appear.

Our main purpose now was to find a way to make our time together as comfortable, practical and workable as possible, whilst also trying to operate as a family as much as we could. Although our world was extremely stressful there were times for laughter with Paul. I had a particular nickname for him (which I will keep for myself and my family) which really made him chuckle and he and I used to go for rides in my wife's car. I make this distinction as the new car I bought for her, the one which mainly stayed on the drive, was one of the old shaped Mini's. I hadn't realised before buying it how much joggling up and down these cars gave you and Paul found it hilarious riding in his special car seat in the back, especially when we drove around the country lanes near our home. I have no idea what his specialists would have said, but as father and son, we thoroughly enjoyed it.

Looking after Paul was a full time job and we were assessed by Social Services to see if we could be provided with a carer to help during the week. My normal perception of a carer would be a woman, great at multi-tasking, efficient, medically competent, warm and kind.

What did we get? In walked this hippy named Zeke, hair down to his waist in a huge ponytail, as skinny as a rake with gaunt features, driving a VW camper van and wearing a type of jumper which had all of the hallmarks of the old Glastonbury festival about it. I thought that this must be a mistake; I would give him a meal, as I was not sure he would make it to the end of our two car driveway before he collapsed through malnutrition, and then he would be on his way.

What did we actually get? An incredible human being. If there was ever a time for the term 'never judge a book by its cover' then this was it. Zeke had all of my normal perceptions of a carer, other than being a man, but these were insignificant compared to the array of gifts he brought to our family. He gave totally of himself, without damaging himself, as he did everything through a love of people. He cared for Paul fantastically, nothing ever a problem. He took Gary to see his mother and their run full of chickens in that VW camper van (we bought Gary one for his 21st birthday many years later) and he became a true friend of the family. Here was a man, easily judged from the outside, who was incredibly comfortable within his own skin. Consciously or subconsciously he understood the true essence of human nature.

Paul's condition started to deteriorate and we began to spend a significant amount of time at Helen House. I shudder now to think that only seven years before our need with Paul, nothing like this hospice existed. We would have been in a mainstream hospital, where without doubt they would have been conscientious in providing medical attention, but they could never have provided the all encompassing care we found in that oasis off the Cowley Road in Oxford.

A Patron of Helen House is the Duchess of Kent. As a family we were asked to attend a tea in her honour, and on the date of her visit we somewhat nervously waited for her arrival. The front door bell rang and the Duchess and her staff started to proceed into the building, only for a 5 year old, with a swerve of the hips that would stand him well for his rugby duties a number of years in the future, to leap straight into her arms. Yes, my son Gary had dodged all those legs in front of him and proceeded to achieve his full on attention grabbing objective of hugging royalty. My fillings were fully visible as my jaw fell to the floor. Mercifully, the whole place erupted with laughter. The Duchess proceeded to ask Gary some questions, still with him in her arms, to which he replied with pure innocence. Having completed his objective, Gary then said his goodbyes and proceeded back through the myriad of legs to re-establish contact with a computer game he had been playing.

On 5th June 1990 Paul was suffering from yet another bout of pneumonia. We somehow all knew where we were and the people of Helen House stayed with us all night while Paul passed away. Heartbreaking as it was, we had the solace that he was no longer suffering, the pain that had recently been with him almost constantly had gone.

What we did have was the collective love of our family. Again the strength and bond between my wife and I enabled us to be there for each other at the various times of need. When one is low the other can encourage and comfort, there is no need to explain why you are upset as the other understands with the same intensity. I now recognise that we were quite conservative people, we did not feel it appropriate to divulge too much to the outside world; in many ways we held back feelings that blocked the senses.

We see examples of grief from the Asian or Muslim community, where there is a huge outpouring of emotion at times of distress, a public display of grief which to us in the west appears to verge on hysteria. Who is right, East or West? Is it right to suppress, show a few tears perhaps, but not fully let our emotions be divulged to the outside world? I now know that the suppression of my emotions from this and other times had massive impacts on my emotional and physical health, impacts that truly surfaced with my relationship split.

Picking Up The Pieces

The lessons of life can be confusing and cruel. Perhaps only in hindsight can we see the true value in events which at the time caused so much distress and anguish.

So what do we say to our children when they can't do something? Try again. When they still can't do it what do we say? Try again. Well, following our traumas of 1990 the family had to try yet again to move forward.

At work I was promoted to Regional Sales Manager. This new responsibility translated into a great deal of travel and hours dedicated to my job. At the time I believed this to be the best policy, get stuck back into my career and continue to push the boundaries.

Over the next 18 months however, I became disillusioned with the business where I had been so successful and I started to look at my next career move. I secured a senior role in a large multi-national company, still within the forklift truck industry, where I had the opportunity to develop two new aspects of their product offering.

My pattern, although I did not really recognise it at the time, was that I continually craved new challenges. After 18 months to 2 years of doing any particular role I would become dissatisfied. This pattern must have been very frustrating for my wife as it manifested itself in the form of dissatisfaction with everyone or everything else, the company politics, lack of resources, investment, ownership or vision.

I stayed with this business for six years and achieved relative success, but again I had become very frustrated and itchy for a change of scenery. I had always fostered a desire to be a Director of a company. I concluded that with this level of seniority I could make the changes required for success, and have the authority and control to complete them. I set a goal that I would become a director of a business before my 40th birthday.

So did I achieve this goal? I missed it by one month, gaining a position as Regional Director with a business that I had known before. The company I joined in 1983, where I became that struggling salesman, had been purchased by a large corporate PLC; Strange to think that I had gone off on a journey lasting 13 years to return at a very different level to essentially the same business, a business with some amazing people.

And who would be my new boss? The man I mentioned who had been tucked away, he in service, me in sales, with his head down just getting on with his job! He had developed immensely and I could feel immediately that our values, outlooks and desires were very much in line. The overall challenge was to develop a business that would set new standards of sales and service delivery.

We wanted to change the rules of our industry. We wanted to demonstrate that by encouraging our people, rather than the traditional model of carrot and stick or just plain outright pressure, we could improve the service delivered to our customers, improve the quality of life for our staff and increase the profitability of the business. Through a great deal of effort and dedication from everyone involved we really started to achieve the goals we had set against a tough trading environment.

I started off in my new role with the normal euphoria I felt whenever I took on my next challenge. The business had appointed another Regional Director at the same time and we started to work well together, shaping out the new structure of the business.

I now had some metaphoric 'stripes' on my sleeve and I must say I felt proud of the position I had worked hard to achieve. However, I found that my 'stripes' were not having the desired effects that I had first perceived. I thought that people within the business would naturally respect the position I had long worked towards; why, had I not in other companies remarked that, "If I had been on the Board we would have got things done"? I was now to embark upon a major stage of my journey.

One day we had a strategy meeting to discuss the implementation of a new IT system for the business. It was clear that the new platform was groundbreaking and provided the business and our customers with fantastic information and a level of accessibility never before available within the industry. The developer of the system, Bob, unfortunately no longer with us, gave me a true lesson in understanding that 'stripes' do not equal respect.

We were trying to determine a timescale for implementation. Trying to tie IT people down to a timescale, I've found, is nigh on impossible. A great friend of mine from Yorkshire once described it as 'trying to knit fog'. In my experience, if you decide for conventional project work that it should take one month to complete then you double it, however, for IT, you treble it at least!

I, as most salespeople will understand, wanted a defined timescale to work towards. It soon became apparent that obtaining a delivery time from Bob was never going to happen. I started to 'insist' that he provide one, as the Board needed specifics not maybe's. The meeting started to deteriorate to a point where my boss called a halt and said we would re-convene at a later date.

I stayed behind in the meeting room with my boss and started to really create about Bob and his stalling tactics, the manner in which he treated his bosses, how it would impact on the business, and any other type of blame I could throw at Bob's door. My boss sat silently waiting until the wind had gone out of my sails, when he then retorted "The problem is you"!

I couldn't believe it. How could he say the problem was me? Bob was the one not providing the business with the information it required and I set off again with another tirade of blame and by now blatant anger. Once the stormy seas started to settle he again retorted, "The problem is you"!

A month later my boss arranged for his two new Regional Directors to attend a one day training seminar for senior personnel, held in a beautiful stately home in Hertfordshire. The day was hosted by the chairman of the training company, one Ashley Boardman, who I immediately felt was very comfortable with himself; not arrogant, just calm, relaxed, confident and easy; the bastard!

The day consisted of a number of activities, the first of which was to complete an eight minute personality profile questionnaire, and we were informed we would get the results at the end of the day.

Next we were asked to present an outline of our company to the other delegates, 12 people in total, who consisted of Managing Directors, Regional Directors and senior account managers. Even after ten years I can still feel the trauma of this experience in my body, how stilted my communication was, how tight my facial muscles were and how I felt that all of the others had presented to a much higher standard than me. But here was the rub; I had aspired for so long to achieve this position as a Director, I had the stripes on my sleeve but in reality I was still working through so many limiting beliefs that I felt like an actor who was suffering stage fright; and I was. I had been acting for many years, believing that I should have attributes like this individual, be able to communicate like that individual, be as detail orientated as another individual, never content with just being me.

The remainder of the day is a blur as I just wanted to run, but, in true fashion, I determined that I could shrug my performance off. 'They' had been so unfair, asking us to do this without prior notice or proper preparation time. For me this would have meant two days of solid preparation in order that I could rehearse and rehearse to cover the cracks.

5pm came with much relief for me, and the venerable tradition of handshakes, 'great to meet you, see you again sometime' took place as we channelled towards the door. Just before our exit a lovely young lady presented us with the results of the questionnaire that we had completed at the start of the day. We all funnelled through the door and headed in various directions to our executive cars dotted about the grounds of this beautiful manor house. I couldn't wait to read what the results said; or could I?

I opened the envelope and started to read what turned out to be one of the best pieces of paper I have read in my life. Eight minutes filling in a little questionnaire, the results of which were thrown into a computer which then proceeded to reveal what I had always secretly known: I was not presenting the real Martin to the world. I was presenting a face, or in psychological terms, a mask that I believed fitted the image I was trying to portray. It outlined that I was altering my personality to the perceived conditional requirements. It further outlined that I strived to achieve my results through diligent analysis while providing irrefutable proof that my conclusions were correct.

Eight minutes of tick boxes inputted into a bloody machine, and I felt my guts had been revealed for all to see. No one else knew of course. I was alone in my car but I knew the results were right. I was staggered and for the first time in many, many years I cried. Sat in my car in those beautiful grounds I started to look back at all the things that had occurred, the struggles, the traumas, the continual striving to achieve goals, getting there and then realising there was yet another door to open. I determined there and then that I had to do something about this situation, but I didn't know who could help or what I needed to do.

I decided to talk to my boss; you know; the quiet one who had sat in the corner all those years ago. Here was another remarkable person I was to find along my journey. I sat with him and talked him through what had occurred on the training course. I now realise that during our conversation my ego was on high defence alert, which stopped me from disclosing everything I was feeling. I did reveal to him however the findings of the questionnaire and as we talked things through I realised that he had an unusual grasp of the human being, a grasp to which I would aspire for many years to come. He appeared to understand what I was saying and was empathetic without being emotional or overly sensitive. He never sugared, or sugars, his words, but he hit me between the eyes with some home truths that rocked my very foundations.

This was the start of eight years of personal searching, knowledge accumulation, the challenging of some of my core beliefs and the unravelling of what I thought was my happy marriage! Up to this point my wife had supported me in every way. Little was I to know at this stage that my dependant needs were, I believe, also fulfilling her needs as an individual. Our son was now 15, doing really well in school, contemplating his O' Levels before A's and University to come, following what is now traditionally know as a 'Gap Year'.

Just as a matter of interest, regarding 'Gap Years', I do not begrudge my son or any of his peers this much deserved break in education for another form of learning. It occurred to me however that the only 'gap' I had taken in my life so far was the one in my front teeth closed by (in my perception) a tyrannical dentist called Mr Chicken!

The PLC we worked for had a very high belief in personnel development and a budget was set aside each year for specialist coaching, training and mentoring. After my discussion with my boss, a piece of this budget was allocated to help me move forward.

I was assigned to an intriguing Yorkshire man called Derek, who had the most infectious laugh imaginable. Many years later I understood, on a much deeper level, that the laughter was an essential ingredient of his mentoring, however at the time I just thought him extremely happy and great fun, which he undoubtedly is too. Derek utilised the practices of Transactional Analysis in his work, which in basic form looks at the behavioural patterns of individuals and seeks to restructure unhelpful reactions to a variety of stimuli.

I visited Derek monthly over a six month period where we started to reveal great chunks of background that were determining my present state, my present way of dealing with things or events and how I was viewing my world.

In general, children up to the age of seven can be seen as porous. They take on board all that they hear, see and feel as fact, all of which then forms into their basic belief system. The child has no fear at this stage other than loud noises and falling. All other actions are without attachment to consequence, so for them going near to a fire, near to a road or approaching a ferocious dog has no meaning to them other than the one which parents condition them to have, normally, as I am sure any parent will know, through a great number of repetitions!

Derek started to unravel parts of my history and how my early 'conditioning' was causing many of my issues. He took me on a special personal journey which enabled me to provide all of the supportive parenting mechanisms for myself. I would no longer rely on other people or resources to give me a framework in order for me to function as an adult. A revelation, at 40 years old, was that so much of my feeling of self was in the hands of others.

Derek also highlighted, during one of our later sessions, how my relationship with my wife would potentially change. He said that as I starting to evolve and deal with my issues, together with our son reaching a more independent age, he could perceive that her natural requirement to nurture would need satisfying in some other way. I discussed this observation from Derek with my wife but didn't feel that she really wished to look into the situation further.

I believe her experience with psychologists throughout her illness with anorexia created a massive resistance towards anything that looked at how the mind operated. The pattern of her introspection rather than open discussion would present itself strongly in years to come, whilst for me, my desire to find out more on the subject of human psychology and personal growth had really been ignited.

I became, I suppose, a disciple of a more positive way of life. I attended seminars by a variety of life coaches, including the 'Fire Walk Experience' with Anthony Robbins, continued to consume large amounts of information, put some of the learning into practise within my working environment, but now I also started taking it home!

Exercise 8 - Conditional Love

This is a cathartic exercise that will enable you to reveal some deep routed 'conditional programmes' you may have. These programmes have the potential to cause some of your responses to your issues today.

We need to bring things to the surface, recognise them for what they were and then choose how to handle them in the future.

Key things that I believe:

- Many people who trade in conditional love have been the victim of this damaging trait themselves.
- Most people do not even know they are doing it; they have probably practiced it for so long they don't know how to operate in any other way.

You can never physically go back and change a time when you were manipulated, but you can choose to look at it now and give it a new meaning, perhaps revealing an empowering alternative behind the deed rather than just the negative.

An example:-

I believe, rightly or wrongly, that an old boss of mine used me in his quest to oust the incumbent Sales Director of the time to enable him to move into the role he coveted. In my naive way, I bought into the propaganda that the current Sales Director was no good, he had lost the plot, he was not up with the times, and many more negative statements.

As a relatively respected person in that business at the time people listened to me, waves were made and subsequently, not just because of me I hasten to add, although I was certainly a contributing factor, the Sales Director was indeed removed from his position and my boss got the role he desired.

A couple of years later I was in real need of assistance from this particular person who I had 'helped' to his cherished position. I made a mistake in resigning from the business, for a variety of reasons, and needed his support to enable me to come back into the company as I knew I had made a significant error of judgement. He had the power to make this happen without any consultation with others. I was staggered therefore when the message I received from him was that '*the management team had decided it would be better for all parties that I was not able to return*'.

As I thought about it then and for a number of years after, I felt betrayed and taken for a fool. I had been used to achieve his objective and then where was he when I needed help? Now, think if I left the story at this point. What are the emotions that surface? Are they not anger, revenge, hurt pride, frustration, spite? Words not found anywhere in the book of positive emotions!

However, with reflection, I can now choose to give this event a very different meaning. I am positive I would not be writing this book if I had gone back to them. I would not have met the same fantastic people on my journey, I would not have grown in knowledge, grown in experience, grown as a person or discovered that I do not have to put up with people manipulating me for their purposes! Does the situation I have described now have a very different outcome? In reflection, I am **so grateful** for their response '*the management team had decided that it would be better for all parties that I was not able to return*'.

Have I deluded myself with my new perspective on this topic? I don't believe so. I believe I have given myself the opportunity to move on from an event where, if wrongly viewed, I could remain stuck for years. Stuck with a damaging frame of reference of that time, stuck replaying that same old film with the same ending, never seeing the real lesson, the real opportunities, that the event was providing to me.

The event will still have happened to you. You will still have experienced the emotions of that time but you can now place upon it a more mature, reasoned explanation that enables you to take control of the event, perhaps for the first time in many years. By seeing the event in a wider timeframe and how subsequent events have transpired to date, you will be able to see an overall picture evolve. This strategy will be of paramount importance later in your path back to happiness and a feeling of control towards your relationships.

- *Can you think of examples where people have used conditional love on you?*
- *When have you felt you have been manipulated by others mostly in order for them to get what they want?*
- *How does this make you feel? What stirs inside you when you remember what they said, or, just as importantly, how they said it? What did they do?*
- *Identify some key examples from your own history and look to see how you can now view the event, widen the perspective, reduce the damage caused and give yourself control of the situation*

The ability, through reflection, to widen our perspective on an event is a foundational Buddhist teaching. It enables us to understand that specific events are interwoven into a much wider picture of the course of our lives. By accepting rather than resisting what has occurred we can gain control and subsequent peace of mind.

The Journey Divides

As a relationship forms, the couple adjust themselves in order to compensate for the differences between them. At some point along the way, these differences begin to show and the decisions made at this point will determine the future path you will have to travel.

Learning something new has danger. If you really start to believe your new found knowledge can help you and other people, it is natural to want to spread it to everyone who will listen. My wife, although not discouraging of my hunger for this type of education and learning, did not appear to want to harness any of the new information and was not interested in using any of it to alter her ways.

Differences between us started to appear more openly. They must have been there all the time but when you are trying to just cope with your own internal issues you cannot always see the external conditions so vividly. I wanted to talk with my wife all of the time, discuss plans, what we could do in the future, talk about anything as long as there was dialogue. My wife didn't see the point of just talking when there was nothing to discuss. We started not to eat together other than at weekends, considering that if we ate at lunchtimes it then did not matter what time I returned from work or if I wanted to go to the gym.

Our life started to revolve around what I classify as events, main items such as a holiday, a family Christening, a work do. Everything else was mundane, nothing spontaneous, living ok at a level until the next 'event', which could be a few months down the road.

We also had another aspect of our life changing, the emergence of Gary as a young adult. When children are young and in need of your attention there is a natural channel for your energy, focus, affection, time, interest and a whole host of other diversionary actions. Now this aspect was changing too. Gary didn't always want to go on holiday with us, he didn't need supervision or day to day support. My wife's role especially had really started to change.

I was still very involved with running a business and by this time had moved into another part of the PLC, taking on my own section of a national company with 200+ personnel, keeping me more than occupied. Although I had moved on at quite a pace I know at this stage I was still wavering between my old outlook on life and my new philosophies and perspectives.

My wife, in my view, likes stability in her life, knowing where all of the pieces are at any one time, and a nice lifestyle. I have described how magnificently she coped with all of the challenges that came our way, however they were challenges forced upon us as opposed to self generated.

The next event that hit us concerned the PLC I worked for. They had decided to sell our part of the corporation to another business. Two months previous to this announcement, I had taken a new position (yes, I had done the last role for 19 months) which, when the sale of the business was agreed, resulted in my new role being redundant, making me the first one out of the door!

Fortunately, I found a role as Sales Director at a competing company straight away and I put my redundancy payment away for a 'rainy day'. Moving straight into this new role we quickly picked up the pieces of a particularly damaged business and started to turn things around. I changed the structure of the sales operation and we began to head towards a result this business had not seen for many years. However, after six months with this company, having once again tasted company politics and manoeuvrings, a thought rekindled in my mind; I wanted to start my own training and consultancy business!

I had spoken often to my wife about doing something on my own but never had the belief or resolve to follow through. Now I was in a position where I had some money in the bank which would support us for six months, I had a tacit agreement with the boss of the company I now worked for to train his senior management team over the coming six month period, I had met a guy at a function who had just started his own training business and with whom I may be able to work with in the future. I decided with my wife that if ever there was a time to do my own thing this was it - I would go for it!

Time for some benchmarks: the year was 2004. I was 44, my wife 43 and my son 20. Gary had completed his 'A' Levels and decided during his gap year to travel to Australia and New Zealand. I can vividly remember, as he walked through the airport departure lounge, two anxious parents with words coming from our mouths of 'go for it Gary', 'have a great time', 'enjoy yourself', whilst trying desperately to cover up that feeling of 'please come home safe'.

At this time my wife and I had holidays together but they were becoming more strained. We had less to talk about, we kept the ship steady, we did nice things. Surely though, this is what happens to a relationship that is now 28 years old, isn't it?

I completed the six month training contract with my previous employer and I also started to work with two people who became extremely close friends, one of whom would become much more than a working partner over the coming years. Nigel had worked originally in the banking industry before starting a partnership with Tony, who had been Chairman and Director of various businesses before concentrating on the business of his first love, training.

Tony is one of the people I am closest to in the world, and the links between our life journeys are almost spookily similar. I am convinced that he came into my life at this stage to help me deal with the coming years of my life, although, thank goodness, I had absolutely no idea of what was coming!

Also at this time we had a fantastic canine addition to the family, I would say again part of life's plan to help me in the future, who has become one of my truly great friends, our dog Harvey.

Over the next three years I managed to find work to sustain our standard of living, however there is definitely a precarious nature to running your own company. Experiencing what worked and what didn't, finding and tendering for new contracts, constructing and delivering the training programmes, ensuring that you got paid and a whole host of other seen and unforeseen factors.

My wife had worked at the local doctors' surgery for 10 years. Now, with the changes within her life, she found herself without a purpose, she did not want to continue working at the surgery and also didn't know what to do for the future.

We looked at the vogue of the time of purchasing property with a view to refurbishment and re-sale. We invested some money in a couple of speculative projects but for one reason or another it never came to fruition. I always felt deep down that there was a real reluctance on my wife's part to really go for it, even though I knew she had a flair for design, could plan really well and seemed to know what would sell and what might struggle. Keeping to a budget would have been more of an issue for her and I said that I would do this and the negotiation side.

I feel she felt lost at this stage. Gary had become independent. I had started this new business with its precarious nature. She was in a role she had been doing for over 10 years. I had also become much more financially focused than at any time previously and I wanted to be involved in what had always been a domain handled by my wife.

I suppose in essence some key gaps had surfaced within our relationship. She had no direction from her own work perspective, people within the family did not need her in the same way now, and massive questions were probably playing in her mind. Questions such as "Where will we (I) be in 5 years time? Am I married to the same man? What have I done with my life?" "Where is my life heading?"

Exercise 8 - It Started to Go Wrong When....

All couples will have differences and the normal method of handling these differences is to modify our behaviour to fit in with each other. Distractions such as children or work dilute, or divert, these differences into other channels of focus, covering them up, in many cases, for years.

It is important to be very honest here. I can see from my own recollections how my continual striving must have impacted upon my wife, who herself continually craved stability and a relatively straight forward lifestyle with little conflict. Likewise, even with all of my encouragement, my wife would not take any steps herself to improve her situation.

These differences thus combined to cause frustration and tension to surface between us.

- *It's 'dig deep' time again. Detail when, in hindsight, you believe you could see the cracks start to show in your relationship.*
- *What started to happen?*
- *Were there any specific events that occurred around the same time that may have influenced the situation?*
- *What were the differences of characteristics between you?*
- *What was your state of mind at the time, happy, depressed, ok, lost, realising a dream?*
- *Think about and document what your individual needs were at that time.*
- *Are your individual needs any different today?*

No philosophies here, just common sense. The recognition of when and what changes occurred will provide you with an understanding of events that lead up to your separation. The key learning here is to accept your responsibility in what transpired. Once accepted, you can ensure that you do not replicate the same situation within your future relationship.

The Event

We try to control the world at our peril. The life we thought was ahead of us can change in a split second. It can change with one sentence "I no longer love you the way I did".

"Great day Clive, fantastic weather, good racing, and the company wasn't bad either! See you soon mate".

It was 28th July 2007 and I had been to a historic motor racing event at Silverstone. Clive has an unbelievable knowledge of the history of motor racing, drivers, cars, teams and events. His ability to show me so many different aspects and details of the highly expensive boys' toys that were being plied with full vigour for our entertainment always astonishes me. Little was I to know that within one hour of that parting my life would be turned completely upside down.

There had been a palpable tension between my wife and I over the previous few days. I had taken some much needed time off work and had an extended weekend of Friday to Monday to enjoy ourselves. On the Friday we had visited a nearby stately home, Blenheim Palace, the birth place of Sir Winston Churchill. We walked the house, attending a guided tour and then strolled through the gardens down to the lake. It felt to me like we were two strangers. There was a distance between us that betrayed any fact that we had been together as a couple for over 30 years. In my normal 'fix everything' manner I asked my wife what the issue was and she said that it seemed strange but that it felt we were just like friends.

After Clive had gone my wife told me that she felt that we were finished and she wanted to leave. I was completely dumbfounded as there had never been a time that we had even discussed a major problem, now here she was saying that she wanted to leave. We spoke most of the night, going around and around the same subject over and over. My chest felt like it was going to split in two, I cried till I hurt. Much of that night is still a blur; the following are my first journal entries that bring many of the feelings, thoughts and fears to light:

NB: I have not altered anything from this or any of the following journal entries as I want you to view the intensity of the feelings I was experiencing at the time. My reflections on these first journal entries are that they contain some practical common sense wrapped around an emotional roller coaster, practical advice to myself tethered by a desperately thin thread of the hope of my wife returning.

Journal Entry - 16th August

I am starting this after nearly 3 weeks of shock. Shock that my wife said she thought she did not love me anymore. I can't even remember how it started other than it was the same day as I went to Silverstone with Clive on the 28th July.

From that day to this my world feels like it is totally upside down / confused / angry but the overriding thing is the pain and hurt inside. I find it difficult to say but this pain seems worse than when Paul died. My main reason for this is that when that happened we still had each other. This time I feel totally alone, sick inside and weak from the stress.

My wife is suffering too against a knowing that what she is doing is wrong but she has a massive feeling inside that she needs to break free. We are at the stage where she is staying anywhere she can but at home as the pressure when we are together is intense.

She has located a flat nearby which she has said yes to for 6 months. I have worked out a plan of how we can pay for it.

Today I saw my wife outside of PC World and told her I had made some decisions. (1) That I did not want to put our house on the market as I had previously suggested as I thought it would be totally wrong for me Gary and Harvey and that if it had to be sold it would have to be for two reasons (a) that there was no chance of us getting back together (b) that we had decided as a couple that it was the right thing to do. (2) That I had worked out a way of paying for the flat.

Today I have had to decide to let my wife follow her chosen path. The thought of this scares me to the bone as I would then have no control of the situation however I have no control now as if I push things to a conclusion there will be no chance of getting back together which is what I desperately want.

When you are not connected to the situation it is easy to say 'you have to let them find their own way' but when in the situation yourself it is paralysing.

My wife said that if she had to make a decision today then she would say we were finished. I can only pray that time will enable this to change.

So what about me? I have to let my wife do this thing. I love her so much and yes it is painful but I want to give every last hope a chance. I have to go along with it and reduce the intensity when we are together. I must not force things and allow the process and time to decide.

I have to organise things for me to do to reduce the intensity of the feelings. I will go out with my sister in law on

Sunday evening; I can look at the pictures to see what's on. I will see my parents on Sunday (that will be hard) I really do feel lonely right now. I realise how much my world was made up of my wife and I am struggling to break the habit but I must.

The intensity of my feelings for my wife has shocked me. I am not sure at the moment if this is fear of loss / soul mate / best friend or routine. All I know at the moment is that I want her to be part of my life until I die but only if she wants it too.

When my wife had the weekend away I prayed and challenged all of the 'higher spirits' to tell me the outcome. It said 'she will come back to me'. When she got back and hadn't changed her position I thought this was the higher spirits not being convinced. However I could be misreading the timescale.

My wife just bought the shopping home and I noticed a distance between us, not by my wife but both of us. Talk was lightweight but when Gary came she did not seem comfortable with giving him a kiss and she seemed already out of mine and Gary's loop. It is strange that from starting this journal entry to now things have moved on. Rather than always forcing everything I am going to have to content myself with just letting things happen, let them take their time and reach a natural conclusion.

I will not resist the process anymore and have committed to the flat arrangements, to my wife not being here often, to making myself go out and just getting on with life.

Journal Entry - 18th August

What a day. I woke up with the picture of my wife with another man at a party and I hit her on the face and walked out. This started a huge stream of emotion much different from where I was yesterday.

I think I am now totally confused about the whole situation. Did my wife ever love me? The flirty bit? Has 30 years gone in 3 weeks? If we did get back together what would be different? Will a 6 month gap really change anything from now? I now feel that if we spend more than the next 2 weeks apart whilst my sister in law is on holiday and my wife uses her house then we know the answer.

Tony called me first thing this morning which was fantastic. Every time I think of those supporting me I want to cry but it is a nice feeling that they are with me.

When you get this tired you cannot think straight about anything. I tried to switch my mind to my job to sort out but I can't focus. I think in some ways my body is shutting down because of the stress.

I saw my parents today. They are extremely confused, my mother is really angry at my wife and she said some things with bite in them.

It's 'funny' sometimes I wonder if my wife is the person I have known for 30 years. Gary said that her voice on the phone was downbeat which lifted me as it might be that she is still struggling to come to a decision or does not want to make the decision because of the impact.

Exercise 10 - The Happening

Try to capture here how you received, or gave, the news that the relationship was finished.

Detail exactly how you felt at that time. Try to unearth the emotions that came to the fore.

I know it is painful, but the pain of burying these feelings and thoughts will hit you dramatically when you look to move on. You have to feel your emotions. I know from my personal experience that receiving the news "I no longer love you the way I did" released so many of my bottled up feelings.

Remember, you are in a safe environment, no one need ever read the thoughts you express to paper, this is for you.

- *Do you have anything you wrote then, or can you write now, about the time when you received your news?*
- *If you gave the news to someone else can you remember what you said?*
- *If, like me, you find it hard to recall anything in particular that was said, think about the events of the day or the place it happened and your thoughts may be stimulated.*
- *What was your immediate reaction? Tears, fury, throwing things, running, relief, stunned.*
- *What did you do? Where did you go? Who did you call?*
- *Write it down and get this memory out of your mind on to paper*

Practical exercise again. Let it all out. Rather than keeping the memories inside your head release them onto a piece of paper. You will feel the benefit I assure you. Do not worry how you write it down. As you will see from my journal examples, this is not a grammar or format lesson this is for you to express everything you thought about that time.

Moving On

It may be a week, six months or 12 years since your relationship split happened so you now have a decision to make. What is the rest of your life to consist of? Is it fair to yourself, or the one you split from, to keep reliving the past? I suggest that it's time to move on. It is time to start your new life and 'you' are about to construct it!

So now is the time to decide if you are willing to take the first steps forward, steps towards the next phase of your life. Are you excited? Are you freaked out at the thought? Do you feel that you have everything together to enable you to view your situation with a fresh outlook? Are you willing to do whatever it takes to realise a fantastic future?

I feel the reaching of this stage of your journey is like watching a TV programme called *'The World's Strongest Man'*. Part of the challenge for each athlete is a requirement to pull a 5 ton lorry along a 50 metre track. From a standing start and with only the assistance of a rope and harness attached to their shoulders, the competitors move the vehicle along the track whilst endeavouring to beat the time set by their opponents.

When we start moving on from the impact of our lost relationship, the effort required to go forward is like trying to pull that 5 ton lorry. The determination needed is immense, total focus is required and, to ensure that you have been following this book so far, all of your exercises should have been completed to prepare you for this very moment.

Hunched low with your knees trembling, you put every ounce of your energy into moving this vehicle forward, and the effort is colossal. You will probably feel like giving up, begin to believe that this is never going to work, think to yourself "why bother" when suddenly you feel the wheels start to turn. Very slowly you begin moving forward, so slowly that it is hardly perceptible, however if you take keen notice you will see the tiny pieces of progress.

At this point you might start to relax and just as suddenly as they began, the wheels stop again. You feel like you have gone backwards, "Oh, what is the use" but what have you discovered? You now know that with the correct effort, the correct strategy and crucially the correct desires, you can move this thing forward. Yes it takes immense effort, yes it takes time and determination but the rewards when you experience the results are fantastic.

Ok, enough of the metaphor, but I hope you can see my point here. Yes, the effort is huge, but if you do not want to live a life of mediocrity, fear or solitude, the only way is forward, and you are the only person who can allow this to start happening.

Do not get annoyed with yourself when you slip. Many months after my separation I still have periods of doubt or worry, but it is how we recover ourselves that is the vital point. We are only human after all, the most complex of animals, but in this single aspect we have our uniqueness as we have reason, we have choice, and you now have the opportunity to choose which path you wish to undertake.

Exercise 11 - The Dream

You are about to enter the most important exercise contained within this book, so now the fun begins for you. "What do you mean 'fun'? Can't you see how hard my situation is? How stressed I am? Now you want me to have a silly dream when all I can see are the walls of my world falling down!"

I can hear you saying these and many more phrases, probably encompassing some expletives, which I want you to really feel. You have a decision to make right now about your coming life. One thing I can guarantee you is this; you are not going to make this decision if you are being defensive!

I want you to create a dream of your future. A dream that brings to life everything you want going forward. Not the mundane things, just getting by, but the 'big' things that bring enormous joy into your life. A relationship you could only have dreamt of, travel, passion, a huge wedding, children, friends or anything that makes you feel really alive. I use the word 'fun' as this is precisely where I want you to come from when you are creating your dream life of the future.

With total certainty, I can state that the bedrock to my recovery, the foundation for finding out who I truly am and the manifestation of my wishes has been through the development of my dream. In bullet point format I will share with you the clean bits of the dream I created for myself:

> *I am with a beautiful woman who loves me as I do her, she is passionate, strong, giving, trusting and family orientated*
>
> *I am a fantastic father to Gary and Harvey*
>
> *I am physically very fit and healthy*

I am confident, internally strong, full of joy every day and very attractive to others

I have loads of great friends and we have huge laughter together

I am a man with a great capacity to give to others

I am doing a job I love and am passionate to share everything I know

I earn great money and have rebuilt my finances to leave a legacy for my family

I have a double fronted house with a gravel drive, a large open kitchen / dining area, a beautiful garden which backs onto fields, a gym and wide open rooms filled with laughter

I drive a car of my choice that feels good for what I do

I am a man of great skill from my life's experiences

I am a symbol of recovery and a better future for others

When I wrote my dream for the future, a month after 'the happening', how close to what I had written was I?

I considered myself a great father, had some brilliant close friends, had life's experiences and a nice car, but overall I was a wreck. If someone was in a room and matching the person against the dream description that I had compiled they would never have found me in a million years! Bags under my eyes, my weight starting to drop off like a stone, unable to work and as for attractive, well, Brad Pitt and

George Clooney had no competition (still don't but what the heck).

What I did know was that I had to have something to hold onto, something that would keep me going when times got tough and something to which, should I start to despair about my situation, I could move my attention and feelings to, that this was where I was heading.

Some people might say that constructing a dream like this is wrong and that you shouldn't play with your mind in this sort of way. You should just see the reality in front of you, don't set yourself up for another fall, after all, this new dream might not come true, things might map out differently, things might change.

I say to you that if you do not have something to focus on that gives you hope, even if the end result is different (I guarantee it will be), my challenge to you is, where the hell are you?

You need something that moves you from a state of fear or anguish, you need something that will give you, when everything around you seems dark, a purpose, a direction and a sense of hope that things will get better.

Map out your dream for the future.

I want you to notice the language that I use in the descriptions and sentences of my dream. You need your definitions to be written in the present tense, as though you have them now, that this is what you presently have or are. Starting each sentence with the phrase 'I am' or 'I have' immediately creates the correct set of instructions for things to begin to come into your life.

Starting your sentence with phrases such as 'I want' or 'I need' is incorrect as this suggests that you currently lack these things, that they are in the future, elsewhere, or distant.

The art of bringing your desires into your life, to attract them to you, is to believe you already have them in your possession. You have to feel yourself there, you have to see you in the pictures of your dreams and hear what you and others are saying.

This method of thinking is an alien concept to most of us, where we judge things only on what we can physically see in our possession. I need you to really trust me at this stage. Think only in terms of all you desire you have right now and you are just waiting for it to materialise!

I want you to establish how the statements you list and the pictures you draw or create in your mind make you feel inside. An energy and pulse will be created by the level of strength of your statement. Visualise yourself actually being what you have written or drawn and again notice how you feel, make the feelings as strong as possible.

As with all other skills that we build, the process of repetition will be required in order to start to bring the elements of your dream into your reality. Repeat the contents continuously in your mind, read your dream description in your journal at least once a day and remove the pieces that start not to fit with your overall desires (you will begin to feel them when they are not right).

Once your dream is established stay constant. Do not keep changing what you desire on a daily basis because this will cause confusion and poor results. This changing of one's mind demonstrates that you have not truly decided what you really want in your life in the future.

I have written out the elements of my dream in bullet point format to provide clarity, however, these can all be encompassed within a story, you can describe everything pictorially, use a combination of the two, or whatever method works for you.

This is one of the most important pieces of this journey, take your time, but please complete this because this is for you and your future life.

The Dream - Part 1

Many people will ask you at this point "What do you want for the future?" and the main answer most of us will give is that we want things to be just the way they were, probably including having our partner back. Dependent upon where you are in your relationship split, your partner may come back to you. We are though at a crucial point in our realisations:

I want you to be very strong here to drill down into these core questions. Again you are writing in a safe environment and the uncovering of these thoughts and responses will provide a picture of what your needs are.

- *Why would you want your partner back?*
- *What do/did they provide for you?*
- *How reliant upon them are/were you?*
- *What would need to be different in the future (remember that the only person you can change is you)?*
- *If unfortunately there is no potential for you to remain together how will you be able to get over this event in your mind?*

The Dream - Part 2

I now want you to put some 'rose coloured spectacles' on and start to think of what would be brilliant in your life of the future.

Take your time to really feel what would make your life fantastic. Be very detailed and clear as this will bring more emotion and reality to your dream.

Don't set limitations on your thoughts. If, for instance, you passionately feel that you want to live near the Great Barrier Reef in Australia, not to escape or run away, but that it 'truly' feels the right thing for you, then put it down. This is your dream, it is for you.

- *Dare to list out all of what you truly want in your life that will bring you happiness and a real feeling of purpose, connection and joy;*
- *Write all of the elements down in present tense and feel the intensity behind each statement;*
- *Put the contents into a story and create a picture board which includes everything you have described, create a song or poem that encapsulates all of the elements of your dream.*

Quantum physics teaches that 'thoughts are things.' We cannot see the energy particles that form from thought but scientists have now proved their existence. A simple example; you think of someone and they call you on the phone. You might describe this as luck or coincidence however when you practice this concept consciously you will realise that thoughts have the power to transform into reality.

The construction of a dream is designed to transfer your thoughts from what you might have lost to a direction of where you are heading. You are thinking consistently about your new life and you are sending a present tense, emotional message, a message that 'in due time' will be answered. The key to success for the realisation of your dreams is to have faith, belief and certainty that what you desire will be received.

Emotional Pain

> Emotional pain is as powerful as any physical wound. We may try to shield ourselves from its effects but running away is no defence. When emotional pain is understood, we can reveal the message that the body is sending to us and more importantly, how to self heal.

Journal Entry - 4th September

I started off very low today. I feel mainly because of lack of sleep. I kept getting wave after wave of emotion and I want this to stop.

This afternoon I saw Amanda my counsellor at Relate. I think she is quite a feisty person. At first I found it hard to talk, continually welling up, but after receiving a huge box of tissues to ease the flow, I finally pulled myself together and we started talking.

She thought I had been extremely acquiescent about the flat. I said I felt I had no choice other than to say yes as the last string would have broken. She asked me had I thought ever about not being in the relationship. I said I had but always wanted to make things work with my wife.

She asked if another man was involved and I said I did not believe so. She asked that if after 6 months my wife said she still wasn't sure what would I do? I said I would know within 1-2 months and I think this is so.

She implied that my wife might be much further ahead in the process of ending the relationship than me and that possibly my wife might be doing the 6 months to ease the impact. This could be the case however this appears calculated, but it is a possibility.

I told her about some of the things I had decided to look at doing:

1. Determine what I want and do it
2. Commit to giving my wife the time, look after myself and let time decide
3. Become the man I want to be – strong, confident, self assured, wealthy, happy, healthy, joyous with life, smiling.

She answered "no pressure there then!"

She then hit me with a statement right at the end of the session that rocked me totally. Having started the meeting in floods of tears, swathed in tissues and eyes still like traffic lights she informed me that 'you do not show your emotions'.

We did not discuss this further as we ran out of time however 3 things have come to me from the meeting:

1. I need to ensure the flat is for the right reasons and not to just go along with things as I had described
2. Is my wife some kind of 'mother figure' to me – is this why, along with her friendship and my feeling totally alone I have felt so desperate?
3. What did Amanda mean 'you do not show your emotions'

I need to let these thoughts wash over me during the next few days. I have to contemplate that we might not have a future and that I will need to start a new life. This is frightening and exciting at the same time.

Here I was, two months into this situation, and out of a total fogbound field a glimmer of light started to appear. Not of hope, not of a reconciliation, not that this had all just been a bad dream, but a glimmer of understanding that my frame of reference, being my wife deciding to leave, was perhaps not what all these feelings were about.

I started to understand that the majority of this situation was about me and the way that I had been living my life to this point. I started to understand that my immense feelings of pain and despair were perhaps based upon something much more fundamental than the event which had triggered them.

Through my studies I had often read that issues come into our lives, sent in order for us to deal with them. When we do not face them we have a tendency to push them away using various methods such as work, affairs, sleeping, exercise, over eating, controlling or submission. When the real, deep down issues are not tackled the pain is, in my word, 'suppressed' inside of us. The pain is pushed to a 'manageable place' where we know it exists but we don't need to visit it very much. It is covered over in the corner like putting the budgie to sleep at night. You know he or she is still alive under the cloak but the chirping stops for just a while to enable you to rest and partially recover.

When we do not tackle the issue, or issues, that our subconscious is highlighting for us the same painful situation will re-surface at another time. This time however it may well be clothed in a different disguise but it will be accompanied by a distinct difference; the pain will be more intense.

Pain is a natural protective reaction and if we did not have a pain dimension or threshold then we would not be able to determine, for instance, that the placing of our hand into boiling water, is an unsound thing to do.

But how do we get to understand this threat? How do we determine that boiling water can have serious consequences for the skin? How do we know instinctively what not to do? We realise this through our experiences and how they have impacted upon our lives to date. Again, think of a child in this respect. In their early days we continually feel like we tell them off all the time; don't touch the cooker, watch out for the fire, that iron is hot, come away from the edge. Children have no fears; they have to learn the consequences through information or experience.

Pain will continue to show up in different ways, through various experiences, whilst increasing the intensity until we have dealt with the unresolved issue. I have spoken about the physical, but what about emotional pain? Recall now the grip of emotional pain in the chest following your relationship split; was it not just as real as physically damaging it in a fall, so painful that you wondered if it would ever abate?

We can look at pain as something we want to escape from immediately, which, in the example of the boiling water, is totally correct. In relation to emotional pain though, rather than the suppression method I had used which was highlighted by Amanda, or utilising the well worn phrase 'time is a healer', I encourage you now to really look at your situation.

As far as possible I have avoided referencing numerous books and quotations as my key objective is to provide practical solutions and give real examples on the subject being discussed. However, at this point I will use a piece from a book called 'Intimacy' by Osho. The following parable from Chuang Tzu caused me to seriously consider how I was going to face this painful situation:

Shadowboxing

There was a man who was so disturbed by the sight of his own shadow and so displeased with his own footsteps that he determined to get rid of both.

The method he hit upon was to run away from them, so he got up and ran, but every time he put his foot down, there was another step, while his shadow kept up with him without the slightest of difficulty.

He attributed his failure to the fact that he was not running fast enough. So he ran faster and faster, without stopping, until he finally dropped dead.

He failed to realise that if he had merely stepped into the shade, his shadow would vanish, and if he sat down and stayed still, there would be no more footsteps.

The trauma of separation was the most powerful level of pain I had experienced in my life. This pain had returned for the third time, first, through my limiting self beliefs, then with the loss of Paul and now the breakdown of my marriage. Through reflection I discovered that these were escalating levels of pain, levels designed to make me change my ways.

When our son Paul died I recall being intensely angry at what had happened in our lives. On one occasion, shortly after his death, I remember jogging down a street in Oxford at night and found myself screaming aloud with such intensity that I seriously damaged my throat. This degree of anger can inflict serious damage on the body, especially if it is retained inside.

The pain I felt for Paul was intense, but in a way it was shared because my wife and I were still a couple. We were there to share each other's grief. When one of us had a bad day, the other would offer support.

With the separation it was completely different for me. Suddenly, for the first time in my life, I had to face the world on my own. For the first time I had to make all of the decisions. I had to accept that I would come home to a place with no lights on, to a home that had suddenly taken on the guise of a house as the essence of the family had been stripped out. My son throughout this period was, and still is, brilliant, recognising where I was and supporting me really well. He though had his own life to lead and, especially during weekends, he would be off with his mates, meaning that I was on my own without work commitments to distract my mind.

For me, the feeling of loneliness was an incredible pain. I realise that many people can handle being on their own well, they travel the world on trips seemingly happy in their own skins, picking up friendships and relationships along the way.

It now occurred to me that I had never really been on my own in my entire life. Throughout my childhood, then into adulthood, straight from my parent's house to my married home, I always had someone around.

The pain I felt from loneliness was the most intense I have ever encountered. For days on end I would cry, not for pity but because I felt that the heart of me had been removed, or so I thought.

My relationship had always been the core of my life. I had never really developed close friendships with many mates to go down the pub with. I am also not a pub type person. I can only describe this as having no problem being in a pub but I would far rather enjoy the company of people over a meal or in a house where the topic of conversation is not football or politics. I am not a rugby playing alpha man, I would rather enjoy the essence and reality of people talking about what is important to them.

Essentially most of our relationships with others involved my wife and me as a couple, a single entity. When the separation occurred this whole situation was thrown into confusion, with some friends not wanting to decide one way or the other, or indeed whether they should get involved or not.

My own close friends are mainly people who I have developed a relationship with through work. In the early stages, this created a difficulty, as none of them lived close to me, meaning that evening's together were difficult or had to be arranged well in advance.

The fact of having no brothers or sisters surfaced with real intensity. People who I perceived would be there for you whatever the circumstance. I would continually be envious of people who had others around them. All in all, with respect to the pain of loneliness, I felt pretty sorry for myself.

I strongly believe that most of us do something about a difficult situation only when the pain becomes too unbearable to ignore. Take going to the dentist. We bite that apple and we get a little twinge, so we start eating on the other side of our mouth for a while whilst it calms down. We then realise that it is starting to hurt on the other side as well so we start putting the apple into a liquidiser to enable us to not have to bite it! Then it happens. You are up all night with raging toothache, paracetamol will not take away any of the pain, your jaw is swollen and your whole body feels dreadful. That's it!! You have got to sort out this tooth! You must get an appointment! This pain is now too much to bear!

Isn't this what we do also in our relationships? We try to patch things up, push the issues under the carpet, only discuss things when an argument occurs and then it all comes out. The proverbial kitchen sink is thrown and you wonder where this mountain of issues has come from, both from you and your partner. Where had these been lurking all this time?

I had reached a point of decision. As the parable quotes: '*The method he hit upon was to run away from them, so he got up and ran, but every time he put his foot down, there was another step, while his shadow kept up with him without the slightest of difficulty*' . I could do what I had always done before and push tackling my issues down inside again. Following the challenge from Amanda at Relate, where she stated that I did not show my emotions, I now realised that for years and years I had pushed my issues 'down into my boots' covering them up and hoping that they would go away, well no more.

I constantly pondered why this feeling of loneliness had such an impact on me. Surely I was an adult, perfectly capable of doing the shopping, ironing, occasional cleaning, paying the bills, putting the vacuum about, cooking, house repairs etc and of course I could easily deal with these.

After months of thought, and frankly despair, I came to realise that my all consuming feeling of loneliness was related to the withdrawal of love from me. I finally deduced that this was not about being alone per se, but that it had its foundations firmly within my interpretation that I was not loved, and this was the reason why I was on my own.

This realisation created a completely different scenario for me than my previous feeling of loneliness. If you think about loneliness what can you do? You can move in with one of your friends, you can move back to living with your parents, you can go off travelling or you can find 'anyone' to fill the gap, you might not really love them but they will do. These are all actions you can take to stop having to deal with the real reason, the 'real pain' that this situation and emotional turmoil is presenting to you to face, and resolve.

The loneliness issue might consciously or subconsciously be (I now know in reflection that it was for me) a key element of why people don't really deal with things in their relationships. We may tackle them up to a point, but in the main we will not move to a position where you may have to turn left and the other person turns right. We can't bear the thought of being lonely, or on our own, because if you are alone you are not loved.

I now had to put things into a different perspective. I now knew that my issue with loneliness was not about being on my own. I now knew it was about the message I was giving to myself that I was not loved. So what to do?

I listed down all the names of people I knew who did love me, albeit not on an intimate level, but on a purely humanistic level. I had my mother and father, my son, my friends, all my relatives, my neighbours, even my wife. I still knew, even though she had decided that we were not to be together moving forward, that there would always be a love that we shared.

This process totally transformed my interpretation of being alone. I now had control over my situation as I had replaced this all consuming thought 'Loneliness = Not Loved' with the feeling that many people did love me, many people had me in their thoughts and that at a different level I was totally connected to them. I now had the power to remove this energy sapping thinking from my mind and repetitiously replace the thought of loneliness with a much more reasoned perspective on the situation.

Does this mean that I am totally happy living by myself? No. I believe that the majority of us want to live our lives in relationships that engage us on an emotional, physical, spiritual and intellectual basis, and the sharing of our life with someone special brings a totally different dimension to our worlds. When one of you is down the other can lift, ideas crackle from little bits of conversation, the bonding of eating together, going for walks, holding hands and simply 'knowing' that the other is there for you are all fantastic pieces of the relationship that can be enjoyed daily, simply and joyously.

What else have I revealed by looking deeply at this topic? I have found out that unless you are capable of living by yourself you will never fully appreciate the beauty of living with another.

This sounds like a paradox, and perhaps it is, but you build a tremendous power inside of yourself when you harness the capability of being on your own. You realise that never again will you be dependent upon another for your feeling of self worth. You know that you have the foundations where, if you had to decide to be on your own in the future, because it felt the right thing to do, you could do it. These capabilities transform you as a person who knows who you are. You know what is right and what is wrong for you. You know you are capable of making the right decisions for you and your partner's future.

If you are affected by this syndrome of loneliness I feel for you, as I know the power of its affliction through personal experience. I also know many people who have been traumatised by this subject. The fear of being on their own has led many to stay in relationships long after they are over, put up with either mental or physical abuse or simply accept that this way of being is ok whilst they ignore their instincts and intuition. This feeling of loneliness is so powerful, so consuming, that people put up with a myriad of negative situations to avoid it at all costs.

I have found living on my own one of the most challenging periods of my life; however on reflection I would not have missed it for the world. I do have days when I scream at my situation and the dog cowers in the corner as my emotions come out. But I know that the feeling I am experiencing is not from a lack of being loved for I know now that I am, by myself and by others. The feeling of frustration is linked to my impatience in wanting my future life to materialise. When I start to 'push' the pressure grows and I just have to remember that things will come at the right time no matter how impatient I get.

We must look for an antidote to emotional pain. The 'pain' is there to tell you something. It is there to provide guidance towards a better way of living your life but it takes time, it takes patience and it takes perseverance to find the answer. What is your reward for finding the answer? In no small way, you will now have the opportunity to transform the quality of your life.

Exercise 11 - Release the Grip

You may not have been affected by the issue of loneliness as I have been, but other areas of emotional pain may have you in the grip of their mercy.

Areas such as the removal of intimacy, the loss of friends, loss of guidance as your partner was the dominant force in the relationship, impacts upon your finances, family ties and many more may be gripping you in a very powerful way.

I would like you to look inside these areas and find the reason and resolution behind the pain. Bring the issue out into the open, examine it and take the appropriate action.

One thing to be avoided here at all costs:

Do not try to brush this subject under the table. Confront these painful emotions otherwise they will always have a massive hold on you. As the parable said:

'The method he hit upon was to run away from them, so he got up and ran, but every time he put his foot down, there was another step, while his shadow kept up with him without the slightest of difficulty.'

- *How has the issue affected you?*
- *What thoughts run through your mind when you think of this subject?*

- *How are you interpreting this situation? Like me are you seeing it as 'No one loves me', or is it leaving you with another feeling just as strong? Keep asking yourself the question and the answers will start to surface*
- *Are you able now to see what you have unearthed in another way? Can you create for yourself a more empowering reference point for your thoughts, one that gives you back the power, control and ability to take action?*

In 'Cognitive Behavioural Therapy' the principle aim is to locate the source of the problem, in order to identify the underlying reason behind the physical reaction that is being experienced. By continually asking yourself questions on the issue, and listening to your inner voice, you will reveal the central element, the central cause. This revelation empowers you with the ability to take the corrective measures based upon the central issue, rather than treating the physical manifestation.

Blame

Placing blame at someone else's door may take away your need to do something about your situation, but does it make the matter disappear from your mind? In truth, it leaves you in the debilitating position of being powerless, rudderless and waiting.

Journal Entry - 1st November

If I sum up my feelings today they would be frustration and anger, frustration with letting my wife go and anger at the financial situation. Not only am I dealing with the loss I am looking at how we split our money and assets and I don't like what I see.

The feeling of anger is I suppose natural but is so far away from what I want to be. I know this takes me back to past days and I can feel in my stomach, my mind and in the stiffness of my body that it is a horrible feeling that really affects me all over.

So, how to change? I have to tell my wife that she must contribute more to the flat. If this means that she has to get a part time job then so be it. I have to get other work to fund this and there appears to be absolutely nothing in this for me.

I have to trust my faith that my reasonableness will come back to me from a different direction but at the moment I feel I have 'MUG' written on my forehead.

Prior to now I have found it reasonably easy to drift into my dreams for the future but for some reason this is different for me at present. I am taking relaxing baths to try to calm myself down, it makes my hair go mad but what's new?

I am meeting an old friend tomorrow but I do not want to be in the state I currently feel, then how to change?

1. I agreed to fund the flat for 6 months and that's what I will do
2. My wife has chosen her path so mine is directly into my dreams
3. I will tell my wife about her contribution requirement next Tuesday
4. I am going to let myself dream this evening about what I have mapped out as my future life
5. I am strong, confident, attractive and loving which makes me feel happy every day
6. I will come out of this a far greater man

All of the reading I had done over the last seven years continually stated the fact of not comparing yourself with others, but it was only now that, whilst experiencing the severest pain, I realised I had been living with a huge inhibitor in my life. This inhibitor, namely me, was still trying to work through my deep set beliefs about myself. I had performed and achieved but the effort and stress were immense, not just on me but on those around me.

Surely though I had not been the perpetrator of this crime. My wife had decided to leave me. I know we had our difficulties, but overall our marriage had been sound, we had dealt with massive issues that life had sent us and had supported each other through them.

'She' had put me into this place of despair and massive pain, 'she' had ripped out my self esteem, 'she' had torn apart our finances, 'she' had placed me in a position of being on my own and 'changed' the whole make up of my life!! Yes, it was all her fault that I am here, and I am going to get my revenge, 'she' will pay!

Take a look at this last paragraph. Can you identify your situation with anything I have stated? Can you feel where this form of thinking starts to take you? How many times can you hear yourself saying words like this, either to yourself, to your friends, your family or your partner, statements loaded with such venom that no serum would ever be able to counteract the poison?

My belief is that this is the position many of us reach after the trauma of separation. I have spoken to many people who have been through this experience who very quickly start to recall the event with such clarity, eloquence, emotion and feeling that you perceive the event happened yesterday. Then you find out that the separation happened 7, 10, 20 years before!

How damaging is this to one's future life, to your ability to form other relationships, to keeping friends that you have around you? Think of someone who always plays the same metaphoric record when you are with them, "Those bastards at ABC company, when they fired me they lost their best asset, I was on the brink of bringing them in their best ever order, just another month would have done it, but no, the bigwigs in the office had their say and I have never got back to the same position again".

How do these things become so ingrained in our memories, appearing so real, that as soon as a tiny spark is ignited related to our 'favourite topic' we are there? Vivid pictures fill our mind, our stomachs start to feel the emotion of the time and physically our shoulders and chest tighten. So, how are these responses all triggered through the stimulus of a single thought?

Our brains are the most fantastic tool kit in the universe with powers we are only beginning to comprehend. Everything that we hear, see, taste, smell or experience is stored in a portion of the Limbic System, the Centre of Emotions. I have no intention of turning this into a science lesson, however, it is crucially important that we understand, in very basic terms, how this incredible part of us operates, in order for us to discover why we find it so hard to move away from emotional reactions that are so damaging to our future lives and health.

The brain is naturally wired negatively as this is a safety device to protect us from harm and danger, allied to the 'Fight or Flight' syndrome. I previously described the number of thoughts we have a day and the number which are negative in nature.

We build skills and beliefs by repeating the same activity, either physical or mental, over and over again until it becomes natural, or indeed forms into a habit and belief that we retain. We do not have to think of performing this 'skill' it is just there for us to use.

When we do something for the first time all of our efforts are focused on the activity. This experience fires an impulse and neuron activity in the brain. As we repeat the action this fires again in the same place, bonding with the first impulse. With every repeated action the neurons fuse further together, eventually forming an immense connection in the brain, the equivalent of a 'steel cable' of knowledge and belief. It has effectively become 'hard wired' into our brain.

Of course, these 'hard wired' beliefs can be very positive. The ability to drive a car, design a house, fly an aircraft, cut someone's hair, write a computer code, sell forklift trucks, comfort a child, perform an operation, all massive, learnt skills and beliefs that assist us and others.

Imagine now how the 'hard wiring' of negative experiences form part of our belief systems. Imagine the emotions that are raised by playing this type of recording over and over and over again in our minds:

Surely though I had not been the perpetrator of this crime. My wife had decided to leave me. I know we had our difficulties, but overall our marriage had been sound, we had dealt with massive issues that life had sent us and had supported each other through them.

'She' had put me into this place of despair and massive pain, 'she' had ripped out my self esteem, 'she' had torn apart our finances, 'she' had placed me in a position of being on my own and 'changed' the whole make up of my life!! Yes, it was all her fault that I am here, and I am going to get my revenge, 'she' will pay!

This way of thinking establishes a route which I believe is one of the most damaging paths to travel for the human being, and I should know because I had done it for years; the path of BLAME.

In my now belief 'Blame' is one of the most powerful, life limiting, emotions that you can be trapped by. The placement of blame provides you with a modicum of relief, an aspirin if you like, a pill that will dull the pain for a period of time. Blame, in general, is directed towards other people. The problem is out there, with 'them'; 'they' have to realise that they have caused this situation and 'they' have to resolve it. 'They' have to change. 'They' must see the damage they have done to me. 'They' must feel the consequences of their actions.

But where does this Blame syndrome leave you? I would suggest it leaves you '**powerless**', '**rudderless**', and '**waiting**'.

Taking balanced actions, for example, the involvement of a solicitor to ensure that you receive everything that is correct on your behalf from the assets that exist, agreeing with your partner that the dialogue you have is on a civil basis or ensuring that the children are informed of what is happening at their level of comprehension, are positive, healthy actions. These are actions which allow you to feel in control and able to move forward. I want you to feel how this line of thinking engenders a completely different set of emotions than the ones running a strategy of "I am going to take 'them' for every penny they have got", "I am going to make 'them' pay in every way".

Didn't you once love this person? What will be the benefit of ending up hating each other? Where is that going to get you in terms of your recovery? Think of the term 'Hate'. How does it feel, light or heavy? Do you really want to carry this type of emotion forward for the rest of your life?

You may feel that I am advocating a submissive stance in this situation. Nothing is further from the truth. I am suggesting that the emotional position of what is fair for both is the correct path. Judge decisions on how it feels inside of you, does it feel right or wrong, is it flowing or resisting, are you fighting or fleeing?

What I am suggesting here is that you have a choice. This is the first element of regaining your power. You have the choice of following the negative herd with a 'hard wired' philosophy most people will advocate. A philosophy that says, 'get even', 'take them for every penny', 'make them suffer'. This is the way the majority of people will view this situation, and why should you be any different?

An aspect of this 'choice' which cannot be ignored is that the negative response will be natural; this is how the vast majority of the world thinks. I have crudely explained how beliefs and habits are formed; now I am suggesting that you should look at things in a new way. A way that will return your power to you, a way that will enable you to feel differently about your current situation, a way that will allow you to take control of the direction you wish to travel. It will take energy and persistence to unpick this steel cable of beliefs inside of you.

At the time of writing I am many months into my separation and I still have to work at these things, however I now no longer feel a victim of circumstance and that makes the effort worthwhile. Are you willing to travel a different path?

Exercise 13 - The Blame Game

My position here is to suggest that there is another way to tackle the syndrome of blame. It will require hard work as you are changing behaviours that are 'natural responses' to the events you have gone through, and you will be resisting responses that most people use.

By making this decision to negate blame from your way of seeing the world, you can now start to recapture the three things you may have perceived as being lost, which are; **your power, direction and your ability to take action**.

With this alternative approach, are you prepared to alter your current way of thinking to enable you to live the life you have always openly or secretly hoped for?

- *What path have you been following?*
- *Can you identify the degree of blame you may have been placing at other people's doors?*
- *Can you describe the different elements of your distress and identify how this makes you feel inside, be it free, angry, resentful or optimistic? Be truthful, as again this is for you;*
- *Decide and define how you are going to alter this situation*

- *What actions can you now take that previously were unavailable to you whilst you were gripped in the negative mindset of blame?*
- *How does this new stance feel?*

Within the practice of 'Transactional Analysis' we have a model referred to as the Drama Triangle. At a basic level, this model describes three aspects of 'rescuer' 'persecutor' and 'victim'. We can be any of these three however if we remain the Persecutor – "it's all your fault!" or remain the Victim – "poor me" we devolve ourselves of the ability to act and take control of our destiny. Fundamentally, we can allow our lives to be destroyed.

Judgement

Imagine yourself standing on a platform awaiting the arrival of a train. As the train arrives you see a distraught woman race to the ticket office, screaming to the attendant that she must get on this train. Armed with her ticket she sprints through the turnstyle, leaps into the first carriage and rushes along the corridor to find a seat. The seat is next to you. Your mind is awash with what is wrong with this woman, why the panic? A death in the family, that must be it or perhaps an appointment with a doctor about a serious health issue, this makes sense. Or she might have a relationship issue and has a crisis meeting with her partner, oh yes, I can definitely see this possibility. You turn to the woman and catch her eye. You feel nervous but out of concern you ask the question "are you ok?" A smile breaks out on her face as she answers "yes I am fine. I know that ticket man can be difficult and as I was late I thought I would make out something was wrong to get me onto the train, works every time!" You have now experienced a paradigm, a different way of seeing a situation.

Another major feature within the psychology of the human being is our propensity to interpret situations or occurrences based upon our own beliefs, values and ego. I hope my message is reaching you now that for you to fully evolve you have to tackle yourself first. You have to understand how you are made up. You have to understand that what you believe at your core translates into how you see the world, but your judgement or interpretation of an event that happens may not necessarily be how things really are.

A term used for this particular subject is a 'paradigm' - the way we see or interpret things or situations.

An example: within your relationship you notice that your partner goes quiet. There feels a distance between you, talk is superficial, eye contact is scarce. You may then start interpreting this in a variety of ways; they are bored with me, they are seeing someone else, the 1 year, 3 year, 7 year, 25 year itch has started!

Your mind goes into overdrive. What about the children? How will I support myself? How will this affect our friendships? Why are they doing this to me? I thought we were happy, am I happy? Who is going to tell mother and father? Questions, questions, questions. We try to work things out, find a solution, find an answer, however the facts are clear. Unless the other person lets us into the issue, metaphorically they open their door, we have no ability to solve this situation. It is owned by the other person and what is going on inside their world.

The mind is a tremendous tool. It can be used to reason, work things out, identify potential solutions and initiate a programme of events. It can also, as I am sure you have experienced, literally drive you mad! The minds mechanism of operation is first to recall past experiences, or, more importantly, your past experiences. It then projects all possible solutions into the future, moving the options backwards and forwards, thus creating different scenarios that enable us to find the answer we are searching for. This resolution process can be difficult to perform on our own problems, now comprehend how hard this can be when you try to solve the issues that are in someone else's mind!

So what do I recommend you do about this situation? You leave it with them.

Easy to say and immensely hard to do, but I want you to think about it. Unless the other person tells you what is on their mind, and often they will not know themselves what is specifically wrong, how can you possibly fathom out their thoughts?

A man will tend to lock himself away in his mind more often than the woman. He will go quiet, moody, short and distant. When he is asked "what is the matter" he responds with "Nothing", immediately triggering the response "you could have fooled me!" A man will often try to figure things out alone, he will not want to tell you his thoughts until he fully understands them himself.

By the time he does offer you the thoughts that have been running around his mind which were "I am trying to think of my next career move which, I know, has an impact on you and the children" you may have created many scenarios in your own mind. In fact, you may well have started to make them make sense, if you understand my meaning. You have lost precious sleep and you have started, consciously or unconsciously, to create a gulf between the two of you, as you have mentally begun to prepare yourself for an event that may never happen. How crazy is the mind!

The more we 'build' a picture of what we think is going on the harder it will be for them to communicate to you. They will be trying to explain their thoughts to you through a set of beliefs that you have started to construct in your mind, thus making it far harder for you to fully understand and listen to their point of view.

A metaphor I often use for this scenario is to imagine two magnets. If you try to push the faces of two magnets together of the same polarity they repel each other. This is the effect you get when you try to force someone into telling you "What is the matter?" You are pushing for resolution and you are trying to force two elements together at the wrong time.

On the other hand, what result do you get when you hold one magnet firm and allow the other magnet to do what it needs to do? It turns around, all by itself, and joins with the other piece simply and effortlessly.

I am not suggesting that this practice to leave it with them is easy. You will need to bite your tongue. You will have to feel a huge love and respect for the other person, often in very difficult circumstances, to be able to allow them the time to come to terms with their issues.

We create so many issues for ourselves by judging a situation through our own beliefs, experiences and values. Your view of life, your own paradigm of reality, can be completely different to the reality of the situation which belongs to someone else.

Exercise 14 - Judge Not

The knowledge that the way in which we as individuals see the world, our paradigm of life, will be different to anyone else on this planet, takes time to comprehend and understand. In the pursuit of understanding others it is imperative that we develop the capacity to listen 'openly' and to truly hear what the other is saying.

This is performed within the practice of non-judgemental listening. A practice which will transform your ability to understand others whilst ensuring you can convey your own needs and perspectives without a prejudice stance to mire the communications.

- *When have you judged a situation in one way only to find out later that what you saw, felt or heard was not the truth?*
- *List down times in your life when you have become involved in judgemental thinking, and be honest*

> *about the outcome. This exercise is very much linked*
> *to the events of your life, and my reason for repetition*
> *is to demonstrate that you now have the opportunity*
> *to evaluate alternative ways of looking at these events*
> *that have happened to you.*
> * *Have you indeed experienced a situation which you*
>   *judged in one way and it transpired to be very different*
>   *in reality, or by now examining it in this new way can*
>   *you come to a different conclusion?*

The very word 'judgement' has a severe resonance. It communicates power, authority and a position above the person being judged. When we judge based on our own beliefs and values we are in fact 'reacting' to the situation, we are modifying what we are hearing and judging it against our own views on life. In the practice of 'Cognitive behaviour therapy' it is essential that we 'respond' to the needs of the other person, based upon their own value system. We provide the opportunity for them to resolve their issues allied to their own beliefs, experiences and goals for life.

Accept Where You Are

> *To fully accept where you are today is one of the most challenging aspects of this journey. Your mind and ego will continually instruct you to do something about your current situation, to take some kind of action, to take some kind of control. The result? A dilemma called 'fight or flight'!*

Each time I come to a different element of the process of 'A journey back to yourself' I recall sayings, anecdotes and metaphors that summarise the particular subject almost effortlessly. I am also constantly reminded through my own resistances that saying something and actually putting it into practice, really walking my talk, can be poles apart. "You are where you are." "Put a stick in the ground." "There's a time and place for everything." "What will be will be" are all easy to say, but when the mind has got its teeth into a subject it gnaws away at you constantly. It churns them over and over again until you end up back in the same place as you started.

Acceptance can appear in the first instance as admitting defeat. It can feel like you are letting things go that you really want to hang onto. Or, you may see acceptance from a position that once you accept 'it' then you become a victim to the other person, that they have indeed won.

My stance on this, in line with my position on Blame, again could not be further from the truth. You accept the situation as it stands today, at this minute, this very second. This is not a capitulation of everything from your side; you have just accepted that this is the position right now.

As soon as you accept where you are now then you bring into your life the opportunity to again transform the three feelings I mentioned before allied to blame, which were feelings of being 'Powerless', 'Rudderless', and 'Waiting'.

I am sure that if you are in the middle of a relationship issue and you are trying to find yourself out of the maze of conflicting thoughts that continuously run through your body, you will want to talk. You will need to find someone in whom you can confide, someone who will provide you with wise counsel, someone who is there for you, not always physically but easily within contact.

For me, this person was Tony, and one day, after many days of discussion, I asked him a question that I was not sure I wanted to hear the answer to:

"Tony, what do you really think about the relationship between my wife and me?"

"Martin, I certainly don't know everything about you two but my views are this. I see a huge gap between what you want out of life and those things your wife wants. You are an adventurer, and although you are going through massive pain and have been dealt a heavy blow, I think you will come out the other side a real star of the future. You need a woman who will encourage your endeavours, be of like mind, allow you both to screw up and laugh."

"Oh, and by the way Martin, don't try to work out why your wife left, it will drive you mad."

The beauty of what Tony said to me that day, 25th October, three months in to my relationship split, have stood me in good stead to this day. He didn't make a judgement about my wife being right or wrong or my being right or wrong. He simply accepted the situation as he saw it, not casting blame, bile or spite around, but rather he provided his perspective on where we were at that specific time, and accepted the current circumstances.

His parting message "Oh, and by the way, don't try to work out why your wife left, it will drive you mad" is, I believe, a profound statement. A statement that can enable us to unburden ourselves from those thoughts which hold us long into the night; what did I do wrong? Why have they stopped loving me? How can they hurt me this way? Can't they see the damage they are causing? Thoughts that are extremely powerful, thoughts which are emotionally draining, thoughts that continue to course through your mind and body, but they are thoughts and questions we are totally powerless to reach a conclusion on.

As we have seen in the section on Judgement, you cannot get into the mind of someone else, no matter how close, no matter how intimate you once were with that person. The fixation to find the root cause of your separation will damage you intensely, although naturally you will go there. The mind will search for answers, for reasons, for solutions, but they are your answers, your reasons and your solutions, not theirs.

So hopefully you can see that the ability to 'accept' where we are is a very powerful position to take. It will provide you with a platform to move on and enable you to start making your own decisions rather than remaining a victim of circumstance. So what is the major block to taking this route forward?

The Hindrance to Acceptance - Ego

So, what is '*Ego*'?

Some dictionary definitions for the word *ego*:

> *According to Freudian psychology, it is one of three main divisions of the mind, containing consciousness and memory, and is involved with control, planning, and conforming to reality*

> *Somebody's idea of his or her own importance or worth, usually of an appropriate level*

> *An exaggerated sense of self-importance and a feeling of superiority to other people*

When my relationship broke down I was left initially with obvious feelings of pain, disbelief and distress, but allied to these were ego based topics such as dishonour, embarrassment, status, and the impact upon our financial status.

The financial distribution is a practical element that requires solution, but it also exposes a huge ego based part of the relationship breakdown, which can further affect us on a very deep level. It can create other 'emotional' challenges such as the type of home you might have to move to, the car you might drive, the holidays you might have or the type of shop that you purchase your clothes or food from.

I use the phrase 'deep level' here in psychological terms. A major activity of the informational working part of the brain is to 'categorise'. This ability to categorise enables us to make fast decisions on a general basis, thus releasing more brain capacity to allow us time to concentrate on the finer detail of the issue at hand. Part of this categorisation process is used to define peer groups, placing people into social structures in order that we can judge them compartmentally. In general terms, 'these' people fit into 'that' category.

From the aspect of ego, imagine that your normal reference is to buy your food at what is widely recognised to be a premium level supermarket. You probably know many of the other clients shopping in the store and enjoy this association during your weekly visit, but then, because of this separation, you have to consider other retailers to provide you with your food. Nothing wrong with the food the other retailers sell, it's just not quite the 'premium level' quality and standard that you have become accustomed to.

You have lost something from where you were. You may consider, or more importantly feel, that your standing in the community has been altered, your feeling of self-worth has been reduced and your pride in what you have worked for all these years has been tarnished. All in all, 'you' are no longer in 'that' category of people you used to belong to.

Advertisers use this ego based conditioning to lure us into wanting products that place us in association with, for example, actors, footballers and TV personalities. We attain these products, prompted by the advert, that then, after time has elapsed and a habit has formed, becomes our 'natural' purchases. These are what we always have or use, our purchasing has become automatic, these products now become what we stand for or project to others.

A great example of ego reaction was displayed in the 1997 film 'The Full Monty'. Gerald Arthur Cooper was the middle class aspirant who had been out of work for months but continued to hide this fact from his wife as he couldn't stand the shame. Meanwhile his wife continued to spend as she had before, as for her everything was fine because he had a good job and they could meet their social obligations, whilst all the time they were sinking further and further into debt.

In a later section I look at how my fears have impacted upon my life to date and provide ways to overcome them. However, I have to admit that before putting them down in this book I really had to think about what I was revealing to the public, or, perhaps more importantly, to people who may already know me (a major assumption here is that people are reading this book but, hey, I have hope!).

I needed to reveal things about myself that had limited me so much in my past. Things that now would be laid out like goods on a market stall for others to see. I concluded that I could not espouse the need to look deeply at your fears without demonstrating, in practical terms, what this meant to me. I had to reveal some of my innermost ghosts to enable you to see how these fears can be tackled, what you can learn about yourself from tackling them and what it feels like to overcome their limiting forces. My ego nevertheless had definitely been challenged.

The ego could be described as 'what you believe you stand for', in other words what others would describe you stand for. Much of how others perceive us is based upon external factors, as previously mentioned, such as cars, houses, what your job is, where you shop and where you holiday.

Now with this separation facing you, the ego has to deal with new, unwanted territory. The ego begins to feel tremendously uncomfortable, 'it' has to take action, 'it' has to do something! A set of circumstances that trigger the syndrome called 'Fight or Flight'!

Fight or Flight

When relationships break down the primitive, automatic, inborn response of 'fight or flight' rises to the surface. Fight or flight is a natural response to anything we define as a danger to ourselves, be this danger physical or emotional. When the syndrome is triggered our bodies immediately start to change in order to deal with this perceived attack. Our rate of breathing increases, our blood moves from our digestive tract to our muscles and limbs, our pupils dilate, our sight sharpens, our awareness increases, our impulses quicken and our immune system increases activation. All of these changes happen automatically, we are ready physically and psychologically to fight or flee from our enemy.

In today's world the need to fight wild beasts on a daily basis is thankfully not normally required, but the same fight or flight response is triggered when we are dealing with trauma, such as the trauma of separation. If we choose to fight, the lawyers continue to become very rich. Our initial feeling of retribution is soon replaced with deeper anger, as the other party then starts to manoeuvre into a fight position also, and so the battle commences. I have spoken to many people about this area, with the general consensus being that this form of assault is the most damaging part of the process. It causes each party to take a harder stance following each sortie, further embedding the bad feeling between two people who once acted as one.

This 'Fight' position alters the chemical equilibrium within your body, causing you to be continually on guard, alert against attack and ready to respond. This preparedness produces, amongst others, the sensations and emotions of tension, stress, fatigue and anger, all draining agents at a time when you need every ounce of energy available.

The 'Flight' response is to flee from the conflict. This may be expressed through the suppression of our emotions, a desire to get things over with as soon as possible whatever the cost, a denial that this is really happening to us or loose ourselves in another area of activity, work, sex, drink, moving away, all with the intent to 'flee' from the pain. As an example, many women I have spoken to, who retain custody of the children, immerse themselves totally into providing their children with all of their practical, emotional and protective needs, perhaps overcompensating for the lack of the other party in the relationship.

They remove themselves from what we might term 'normal life', if that does not seem unkind. These women, because of the immense pain they have experienced and because of how their ego state has been massively affected, withdraw into the nurturing of their children, and forego their own needs and desires.

An outcome of the massive changes that the body experiences when subjected to Fight or Flight is that our ability to react in a calm, practical and useful way to the situation in hand is greatly diminished. We have become primed for action, primed for attack. Rational thought greatly diminishes, and the possibility of an irrational response is significantly heightened. The scary thing when looking at this situation is that this response is inbred, it is natural to us as human beings, it is a part of who we are.

Now that you are aware of how, as humans, we have natural responses to the stimulus that we experience, your awareness to what is occurring should be heightened. To assist you further, I have detailed below a simple relaxation technique. This can be used to 'calm' yourself whenever you feel the build up of the 'Flight or Flight' syndrome.

Relaxation Technique

1. Focus on a word or phrase that has a positive meaning to you. Such words as 'one', 'love' and 'peace' work well. Short phrases such as 'Lord grant me peace', 'I am calm', 'I am love' can also be effective in quelling the physical changes within your system and cooling the mind.

2. When you find your mind has wandered or you notice any intrusive thoughts entering into your

mind, simply disregard them and return your focus to your word or phrase you chose.

3. Practice this for 15 minutes, twice a day. Practice at times when you are not stressed in order for you to build the skill and experience the feelings of calm and focus that return to you.

Exercise 15 - Is that My Ego Calling?

Allied with this understanding of how your ego may be influencing you, the art of 'acceptance' is a type of drug with massive blessings. Something so simple however is rarely discovered until you are placed in a position where the pain is intense, where you have been brought to a halt, where you are made to look at where you are in your life right now.

When I reflected on my own situation I could see that I had an unquenchable thirst for more 'things' in my life. I was constantly looking at the next step in my career, the next home, the next car, where our relationship was going, the next holiday, the next event, etc. I had not accepted that what I had was great, to be enjoyed, to be savoured, I was just looking at the next goal.

Be easy on yourself now. Accept where you are right now without attempting to fight or flee from the situation. This is where you are, and it is only when you come to terms with this, when you can stop the ego voice inside, when you listen to what your heart is telling you, that you can truly begin to move forward.

- *List down how you think your ego could be getting in the way of you making progress*
- *What are you resisting, what are you fighting?*
- *What are you stopping yourself doing that the 'you' inside keeps telling you to do?*

- *How would you feel if you let holding on to old statuses, old judgements, old habits, old ways of thinking go?*
- *You are where you are now. List down what feel right for you moving ahead, not what your family tells you, not what your friends tell you, but what feels right for you?*

The art of acceptance in Eastern philosophy asks that you accept where you are without judgement of whether it is good or bad. In their phraseology "it just is" that this is where you are today. The control of the mind is central to this practice. The mind continually looks into the past for reference material and then tries to map out the future, but it only knows what it has learnt, therefore it can only repeat what has already occurred. The residue of this continual examination leaves us in a perpetual state of longing for somewhere or something else.

Living for Today

After you have accepted where you are, it is essential that you start to understand how to maximise your life today, to live every minute as though it could be your last.

Having reflected upon many aspects of the way I had been living my life, I began to realise that in the main I was rarely present. My description of being present is to truly be here in the moment, to be, to have no other thoughts other than being totally focused on this time.

An example: can you recall a time when you knew that another person was totally listening to you? Their full attention was concentrated upon your every word? You sensed that they were soaking up every syllable, every letter that you said, they were totally there with you? It is beautiful, is it not?

The majority of the time most of us are not present. Whilst trying to listen, we are making all sorts of assumptions, decisions and judgements about what is being said by the other person, in order to enable us to respond at some time. We reference from the past, or more precisely our own past, for links to the subject matter in hand. If the listener has been through a similar experience, as in this case a relationship breakdown, they will bring all of their experiences to the forefront of their mind, some of it useful, other parts not, but the principal thing is that whilst they were accessing these memories they were not fully with you, they were elsewhere.

I realised at this point that for most of the time I had been continually searching for something else, whilst my wife reflected very much upon the past. This difference of reference points creating a void between us.

The main result of this 'non present' syndrome is the creation of dissatisfaction with all we have. What we have is never enough; we are always searching for something else. I know that I hankered for the recognition of status, achievement, cars, money, holidays etc and my pursuit led me to miss out on much that we had achieved.

Once there on holiday I was planning the next day's action. Did I really taste the food and wine at the restaurant we were eating in at the time? I don't think I did. Did I truly experience the grandeur of looking into the Grand Canyon, with its amazing colours and rock formations? A memory, but one I know could have been ten times more powerful if only I had allowed myself to just be totally in the moment.

I now realise that accepting where I am, and squeezing every piece of enjoyment from the day is the principle of how to live. A principle that is not always easy to achieve, but things that are really worthwhile never come easy at first, but the prize at the end is magnificent.

Living in the past takes us into the world of our experiences to this point, a world we are powerless to change. Reflecting on all of the things that have happened to us, re-feeling the emotions of those times and recalling over and over any hurtful or aggressive things that people have said to us, lock us into a hell that we drag around with us all day long. Tell me now; have you ever done this and how did (does) it make you feel?

Living in the future can bring about another living hell. It is fantastic to dream, create for yourself a destination you would love to arrive at and set off on your journey. But, if your happiness is linked only to your dream and you haven't enjoyed every day on that journey, you will arrival at your goal and think; "Hey, this place I have reached is not as good as I thought it was going to be, oh well, I am sure tomorrow will be better anyway" you will remain unsatisfied. You will still be searching. You will be unable to taste the sweetness of what you have achieved. Your continual feeling will be one of dissatisfaction, dissatisfaction with what you have today. Your happiness has to be in this moment, now.

There is nothing wrong in my opinion with desiring 'things', setting goals and working towards a better future. The 'wrongness' is when we lose sight of what we have today and when we use dissatisfaction as our driver towards tomorrow. This continual feeling of striving, continually working at something, leads us to a life that can never be satisfied.

Back to those sayings and metaphors, 'Tomorrow never comes'. Accept where you are today and let the stress of the past and the future ebb away. This is one of the most challenging elements within this journey and I admit that I still, after many months, have to continually remind myself of this practice. However, when I can live with the acceptance of 'now' I then feel in control, I feel relaxed and excited by what is to come in my life, enjoying today and whatever it brings.

When I live 'now' I feel like a child again. As a kid I remember leaving the house in the morning, disappearing for the day, being completely engrossed in the activities of playing football, war, wellington throwing, wading through streams, stone fights across the gardens, being chased by the local farmers. Never a worry about tomorrow, that would sort itself out.

I tell you, crack this topic and your life will never be the same again, I promise you. Become a child again. Yes we have responsibilities. Yes we have to ensure that we are not ignoring what has to be done but just feel for a moment that release when you think again of yourself as a child.

It continually amazes me that we can see, hear or experience something over many years but at a different place in time their meaning, to you, is significantly different. After my relationship split, the lyrics of songs took on a completely different significance to perhaps the superficial meaning I had previously related to them. A song that encapsulates so much of what I feel is allied to the power of living for today, is by Mike and the Mechanics, called 'Sitting on a Beach of Gold'. The lyrics summarise the whole scenario surrounding living outside of the present moment:

'I didn't know when I was lucky, discontented feeling bad,
Filled with envy for possessions other people had.
I found my pride had always hurt me, fought the world to gain control,
Not realising I was sitting on a beach of gold.
Oh Lord, I'm a poor man with all the riches I can hold,
I'm a beggar and I'm sitting on a beach of gold.
The problems I encountered, gave me strength helped me sustain;
To know the pleasure first I had to cure the pain.
When I was searching for solutions I found the answers lay in me,
I'm a drifter but I'm drifting on a silver sea.
Are you out there now on empty, feel you've nothing left to give,
Sick of trying, have you lost the will to live?
Don't be drowning in the shallows with the beach so near at hand,

Hear the voice say, get up, stand up and join me on the gilded sand'

You now have the power that you can make the choice of accepting today as your current position. You have the power to create your new future direction, decide where you want to go, have what you want to have (Have you completed your dream exercise yet? If not go directly to jail, do not collect £200 and start writing!)

You have the power to act now; no more waiting, no more feeling the victim of circumstance, no more feeling that everything in your life is being determined by someone else who has said that they don't want you anymore.

Exercise 16 - Past, Future or Present

The main benefits we can take from the past is the learning and lessons it reveals to us. Looking towards the future can provide us with juice and sustenance to keep us going, to give us hope of a better place or time to come.

I want you now to investigate if you are a Past, Future or Present person. I want you to uncover the effects that this reference point has had on you and your relationships.

If you determine that you are you a '**Present**' person, always living in the now, feeling totally tuned in to exactly what is occurring at this present time and not looking to the past or the future, I would suggest, you are truly blessed.

- *Do you feel you are a 'Past' person? Do you always refer to times when things were good, the music so much better than the current tuneless ditties, summers were much more consistent than today's erratic weather conditions, you looked so much better when you looked in the mirror then than now?*

- *How do you feel this reflective nature impacts upon how you view your life, and especially your current situation?*
- *What thoughts do you continually run around your mind? Write them out, can you see how they might be affecting the way you are seeing things at the present moment?*
- *Are you a 'Future' person? Are you continually looking to the next challenge, hoping that tomorrow will bring you contentment and the rewards you deserve for all of your efforts?*
- *How does this continual searching truly make you and those around you feel?*
- *Does it in any way detract from enjoying the fruits that you have today? List out the things you are searching for; are they necessary? Where will they take you? Are you missing what is great at this present time?*
- *Whether you are a Past or Future person, I now want you to describe how you are going to move yourself into living for today, living for now. Look at things through the eyes of a child. What joy can you bring into your life today that will make you smile, feel good inside and feel contented? There does not have to be any cost or any other person involved in this accomplishment. A walk in the park or woods. 'Really' look at a bee circling a flower .Listen to a fantastic piece of music. Truly enjoy walking the dog. Kick a ball. Sing at the top of your voice (definitely done on your own!) Go on, try it, live today.*

A practice widely used in the coaching of individuals, is to uncover whether they live in the past, present or future. People stuck in the past, re-living memories, normally negative in nature, or people continually striving towards the future, create mental experiences for themselves that divert them from the position of now. Once people are made consciously aware and understand their reference position, new choices can be made, allowing them to move towards a position where yesterday and tomorrow do not distract from enjoying today.

Rain Check

Let us stop for a moment to reflect on where we have travelled so far on this journey, we have certainly covered some ground!

Time for a deep breath. Whilst travelling along this journey back to yourself, it is important to take some time to reflect on your progress. You have removed the lid from many areas of your life that you may have wanted to remain covered. This steaming stew of compounded events, your history to this point, you have now dissected to reveal the hidden gifts that have always been present there for you to use, present but possibly not understood before this time.

You have detailed why you were first attracted to your partner and what it was about them that made you feel the way you did. You have looked at the events you faced together, how they shaped you as a couple and what they revealed to you about each other.

You will now know yourself much clearer. You will know how you are affected by conditional love, how your past experiences have altered you and perhaps moved you away from the person you want to be, you have described the unravelling of your relationship leading to the time of separation and you will have recalled the level of pain associated to this culmination of events.

Whilst undertaking this journey to recount your history, with its revelation's and learning's, you reached a critical point where you chose to enter the world of recovery and hope. You crafted and shaped a dream of your future life. A dream that gives you pictures, sounds and feelings of all of the things that will make your life rich, exciting, joyous and purposeful. This is a dream that gives you direction, a dream that maps out your new life path and a dream that gives you a focus for your mind when times seem dark.

You will now have a better understanding of why thoughts have tremendous power, a power we can harness to bring about anything we want in our life. Through the escalating degree of pain associated with our life's events, you will have gained an insight into the physical manifestation of emotional pain and how this is sent to encourage us to change our ways. As the song stated *"To know the pleasure first I had to cure the pain".*

You have had the opportunity to accept where you are at this particular time, an acceptance of your position without judgement of it being good or bad. You will now be more conscious of whether you have a disposition to live in the past or the future, with its distraction from truly enjoying today, whilst your elimination of blame, revenge and ego from your decisions have enabled you to look at the world through a new set of eyes.

Your current position is this; ahead of that very important first date, you have been meticulous in your preparation of the clothes you want to wear. Your decision now is to determine if you have the guts, stamina and desire to put on these clothes, to leave your house and walk through the door towards your new life? Are you up for the challenge?

Facing Our Fears

> *Our internal fears can limit our lives dramatically. They hold onto our ankles each time we attempt to participate in something we would really love to explore or they damage our possibilities for living the life of our dreams. Looking these fears in the face, confronting them for what they truly are and taking action to overcome them, release us to another level of joy and personal fulfilment.*

At this stage of my journey, having learnt so much about myself and how I had reached this point, I began to allow more empowering thoughts and disciplines into my daily situation, but a whole new raft of issues started to well up inside of me. Issues, I again knew, which I had suppressed for many years; my fears came into my mind to haunt me as never before!

Journal Entry - 3rd November

I have been up 2½ hours so far today, and have been through so many emotions already. The most powerful of these is anger. So what am I angry at?

    1.   My wife's rejection of me from her life

2. My having to push things like meeting up with people just to get out of the house
3. Not knowing if I will find someone else, do I want someone else, where and when
4. Living on a day to day basis
5. Struggling to understand what my destiny is
6. Tackling all my beliefs and fears
7. Not being in control of my emotions

Having listed down these things I realise from my learning the following:

1. I am trying to control things rather than knowing what I want and letting it go to come back to me
2. I still love and care for my wife but we were not happy as we were – I am not sure the way things have been done is right but my learning's tell me that things happen for a reason. I have always tried to sort things out before and this situation has stopped me being able, physically, to do anything but support. I realise my wife is in tremendous pain doing what she has done and I hope her rewards are worth it. I had to stop whilst writing this as the thought of my wife being happy with someone else is hard to accept, however if I am to look at this from a higher level then this is the position I need to accept and be comfortable with.
3. I realise that angers (2) (3) (4) (5) (6) are all linked to my journey and in essence are things that I have thought about for a long time but not tackled. I had said so many times to my wife about my lack of local friends. Brutally I have now had to tackle this and I am proud that I have managed to do it. Again, I had raised the issue with my wife of going dancing *[more of which later]* brutally I have faced this and

continued, and will continue to go, because it is a great way to meet people, is energetic, fun and I can be someone invisible if I like which at present is great.

In my moments of low the situation regarding others comes but I think this is also linked to my disengagement to my wife. If I hated her then this hate would possibly drive me but my essence is that I will find someone who also has a broken heart and we can mend them together. I need to ensure that the person I meet has the growth, drive, and open mindedness to allow the relationship to develop onto a much higher plane once the healing has begun. I need to trust that the person is there for me now and at the right time we will find each other.

Living on a day to day basis. When I wrote this down I smiled as of course this was one of my worst traits before the happening. I know I am still not making the most of every day but I know I am living in the present tense.

My destiny or purpose in life is not yet clear however I believe I am in the healing process of me before I can move onto the next challenge. I outlined the other day that my core personal skills were in materials handling and psychology / coaching.

Tackling my beliefs and fears. I think my beliefs through my re-education have remained pretty constant. I am driven by love and want to share this with everyone. I thought this separation would make me bitter but other than the odd occasion my philosophy on life remains: treat all as an equal; everyone is special, share everything I know with those who need it, none of which have shifted. Tackling my fears on the other hand is a longer process. I do think though having listed down my current major fears letting go, showing off, my height, lack of memory, finances, people not liking me, attractiveness, my hair, I can see how these things have held me back and by tackling them I will get so much back to power me forward.

In some ways my not being in control of my emotions, my anger, is the worst one as this was a major block that has been released by this situation. My 'pushing my emotions down my boots' days are over and I will feel every experience and not hold back from letting it show. The release of my emotions was long overdue and I will never suppress them again.

In the continual pursuit of releasing our emotions, it is vital that we do not 'push down, push away or suppress' the issue or issues that are concerning us. You will notice that I come back to this subject time and time again because it is, I believe, at the core of most of our personal limitations, conflicts and negative behaviours.

Pieces of our personal make up, such as our fears, have within them a gift for us to learn from and use, but we will only receive this gift if we have the courage to look them square in the eye and confront them. Our fears have polarities. Allied to the principle of pain and pleasure which prescribes; we cannot know pleasure if we have not experienced pain, we cannot know the light of day if we do not experience the dark of night, we cannot know what it feels like to be relaxed if we have never felt stressed, our fears are what we would really like to do or be on the other side.

I realised that the issues, or more precisely the fears, that kept jumping into my mind were things that for many years I had known or pondered about. Fears which I thought were easier to push aside rather than deal with. I had diverted my energies into other, 'more meaningful' activities, anything that utilised my available time rather than face the major blocks that were preventing me from moving forward. Now, through this separation, all of the opportunities for distraction or denial have been removed. I had been thrown against the wall so hard that it had released my fears in such a powerful way that I had no choice other than to tackle them head on.

My List of Key Fears:

- My height
- Showing off
- Letting go
- Lack of memory
- Finance
- People not liking me
- Attractiveness

I will not bore you with a written examination of each of my dominating fears, but I have detailed a full example of my deliberations and conclusions on the subject of my height to demonstrate how I reviewed the topic and ran through it to find a helpful resolution.

Once I started to dig into each fear it became very evident that the initial description, for example my height, was not the core problem, it was in fact an offshoot of a more fundamental fear.

Journal Entry - 4th November

My Height

A fear or hang up of mine is my height. I am five foot six and a half inches tall, that half inch makes all the difference, and although it had been a latent issue for me over the years it now appears immense. I feel that I am comparing myself against everyone else and when you are looking at something in a certain way you find that everyone is taller than you!

On reflection, this fear has created a belief in me that forms part of the reason why I feel I have struggled so much to this time. I thought that this was a hindrance to the development of my career, to the style and type of clothes I could wear, but especially in view of how other people saw me.

I really have to look at this issue. Why is it so acute? I mentioned it to some people who had known me for 20 years and they said that they never even thought that I was short. On my daily walks in the woods with my dog Harvey again and again I have pondered this subject.

They say that once you bring your fears out from under the carpet, or whatever metaphor you wish to associate with this subject, the fear starts to diminish. You bring it from your subconscious to your conscious thoughts, enabling it to be worked on by the mind. I have found that the resultant outcome of this issue is not what I thought the answer would be.

I have realised that all of the time I was wishing that I was taller I was building a belief in myself that I was not a good person because the world was taller than me, they had it better than me, they would get better positions than me, that in fact they were more attractive than me! Now I have found the real reason; attractiveness, this is the core of the issue.

Here I am at this stage in my life without a relationship and something that had been festering within me for years is suddenly right on the surface, right in my face where it needs to be tackled full on.

It is one thing to identify the core but what do I do to resolve it, how can I handle the issue?

The first thing that I have to realise is that what you are as a person is what is important to others, not the height you stand above the ground. I bet anyone reading this would say 'but of course it is the person rather than their stature that matters' however when you are the person in question and you are looking at the world as I have been, then the belief on the subject is very different and it will take continual re-aligning of my thoughts to move forward.

It is interesting though having thought about this fear how external influences play a major part upon our perceptions. You hardly ever read an article about Tom Cruise without them mentioning his height, as though it is something bad, something to be ashamed about. Well, I think old Tom has done pretty well for himself, in terms of his career, his earnings and especially the ladies he attracts. I think I am going to keep his success in my mind every time I have a height hiccup.

With now being aware of this situation, having now realised that it is linked to my attractiveness and not the physical height I am, I have noticed in reality that there are a lot of guys of my height, but there are many shorter and many taller.

I have also noticed that many of the ladies with men of my height are about the same size as the man. I have also found that I am more attracted to women of this height than those shorter than me, funny this.

One thing is for sure: I am never going to change my height. I have to learn to embrace it and make it part of me. When I look back it has not stopped me getting any work position I have focused upon, I just thought it was harder but in reality it was not, it was just how I was thinking of the situation.

I think the lesson from Mr Cruise is an important one for me, I can use him as my reference point and I am really looking forward to attracting into my life a beautiful woman who will be exactly the right size for me.

A key part to this process is in the recognition of the 'real' issue. Once you know what is really driving the fear you can start to put some perspective into your thoughts. You can see how the issue weighed you down, pulled you backwards and possibly, in this context, how it impacted upon your relationship.

To change deep set beliefs takes time and effort to bring about. In some ways I am quite pragmatic. One of my best friends Nigel once said I was like the disciple Doubting Thomas, who needed to actually see before he would believe that Jesus had risen, he would not just believe based upon what others said. I realised that for me to install a new belief I had to put reality into my reasoning. I altered my belief to allow me to feel comfortable with the instructions I was giving to myself. Yes, many people are taller than me, but there are many people shorter and there are many people of my size around. The core belief on this subject that I have now installed is that we are all great people, irrespective of what our physical status is.

I found that the releasing of this major fear for me was a cathartic experience. I realised that all of my issues lay in ego. I had been comparing myself to others rather than being satisfied with the incredible person I was and am. All the time I had spent wanting to be taller was time totally lost on a subject that I could never truly change (outside of a torture rack or more platform boots from the 70's).

I will not write here that I am fully resolved in this belief. I do still find myself comparing myself with others, but I can now smile when I realise I am doing it, for I know I am now in control of this fear rather than the other way round.

Exercise 17 - What Are Your Major Fears?

Take time now, perhaps for the first time ever, to write down what your fears are.

Go into detail, where you think they come from, but most importantly, how they affect you within your relationships.

Be really honest. No one need ever see this list except you. You may start to realise and release hidden 'monsters' that have been holding you back for a very long time. It is difficult to confront these fears, to challenge issues that may have been lurking within you for many years however, along with the creation of your dream, this is one of the most rewarding things you can do for yourself; as long as you are prepared to act on what you identify.

- *List down your fears and then highlight the top five. Just concentrate on these, or choose one which, if you dealt with it, would transform your life.*
- *Examine the core of the fear. Are you describing the fact, or cause, or are you describing the effect it is having. The effect is where the answer lies, what it is making you do, how does it make you feel, where does this come from?*
- *Keep asking yourself the questions and the answers will surface*
- *Document your findings and then determine how you are going to deal with each fear moving forward*
- *Do it!*

> *Quantum Physics teaches us that thoughts are things. The brain uses repetition, either physical or mental, to build up skills and knowledge. The continual production of powerful negative thoughts about our fears drives them deep into the subconscious. Using the practice of 'reframing' from Neuro Linguistic Programming, we can review each fear, search for their inner meaning and then alter the conclusion, thus providing a positive reference point rather than one that limits our future.*

Interpretation

> *Retained memories of our experiences leave us with feelings, thoughts and beliefs which can be good bad or indifferent. By consciously choosing to review how we are interpreting a negative event, we can expose a new meaning that may have provided 'just what we needed' at that specific time.*

Journal Entry - 27th October

Well the test continues! Today was the remembrance service for Helen House and I was determined to go. Gary came with me to Oxford. On our way I was hit from behind at a junction, putting my car off the road. In isolation this is no problem. The key thing is that Gary is alright. The people who hit us were really nice, very apologetic, a guy about my age and his girlfriend who was driving. It is however just another thing on my to-do list.

Journal Entry - 29th October

A couple of weeks ago I started to pose the question in my thoughts for the future that I would like to meet someone who was dealing with the same situation as me, lived near to my home, who potentially could become a friend and we could do the 'looking' together. Well, the couple who ran into the back of us on Saturday, I spoke to today. I said this would seem crazy but I explained my situation and the guy said he had been going through a divorce over the past year and had the scars and bruises to prove it!

We are going for a drink on Sunday evening. Now it is strange. Did this accident occur to bring him or them into my life? It puts a burden on other areas but I think it will be worthwhile.

I am sure that everyone reading this book could write a list, in double quick time, about all of the unfortunate things that have occurred to them during the course of their lives so far.

It is estimated that 6.7 billion people exist on planet Earth today. The statisticians believe that the global population will have grown by a further 3.5 billion to a staggering 9.2 billion people by 2050! Even if these figures are high or low, the fact remains that each of these people will have a unique face, a unique set of fingerprints and, just as importantly, a unique mental DNA which is the result of their life experiences up to this point in time.

As mentioned within the section 'The Hindrance to Acceptance - Ego', in order to free up our brain processing speed, a portion of our limbic system 'generalises' the information we receive. This generalisation compartmentalises large chunks of this information which, because of our beliefs and references, we can accept as fact. This 'chunking' creates the brain space to allow us to concentrate on the specifics of the task in hand.

As an example, according to statistics, there were 270,000 marriages in the UK in 2007, there were 150,000 divorces, and marriages were lasting on average 11.6 years. These facts can be accepted by us as they come from a qualified source, but is this all there is to these statistics?

As a further example of how we generalise and deal with events that occur, imagine that you are watching the news on TV. One report describes a massive earthquake somewhere in the Asian continent, potentially killing and maiming thousands of innocent people. Thousands of homes have been destroyed and there is no clean drinking water available. You empathise; you say how dreadful it is and then you carry on with your day. As previously arranged, that evening you go out for a meal with good friends, all as though nothing seemingly has occurred.

Imagine however, that you had family in that part of Asia. You would be panic stricken; frantically you would try to make telephone contact with your loved ones in the country itself. If you could not make direct contact you would be calling other relatives to see if they had heard anything. You would be glued to the television news channels to obtain the latest update, trying to pinpoint exactly where the most affected areas were. Go for a meal with friends? Your life would be upside down, your emotions would be fired with anxiety, fear, despair and thoughts of the past and the future. Your mind would go into overdrive, dwelling on the ramifications of what would occur if the worst case scenario has happened. Go for a meal with friends?

You then receive the telephone message "All of us are safe, the disaster happened 200 miles away, we have been watching things unfold on the television". Suddenly, you feel instant relief. You still have empathy for the people who have been affected, but the emotional association, the emotional connection, is massively diminished. Your body stress starts to cool down and ebb away, your mind changes from complete turbulence to relative calm, 'your world' is now ok again.

It is vitally important to understand that all of these rushes of emotion are created inside of you. They are triggered by your interpretation of what 'might' have happened. You may have no real evidence to support the thoughts but the mind runs away at a colossal speed. It fires up your body in response to a stimulus created by you seeing or experiencing something that had an association with you as an individual.

Now, armed with this knowledge, you can begin to understand why you can't just shrug off your relationship breakdown. You are not a statistic. You are one of the most complex animals on Earth. You are an individual with memories, connections and complex emotions. The status you hold on this earth gives you the power to achieve anything you want, but it is for you to choose the route. The way in which you interpret your experiences can set you off in a direction where negative or positive emotions lie. You have the power to choose the direction, towards your empowerment or detriment?

Exercise 18 - Look At It This Way....

When in the grip of an emotional nightmare, such as a relationship split, it is difficult to cultivate the perspective that there may be a different way to view the event or situation you are experiencing.

I want to encourage you now to start looking at 'things' that have happened to you recently in a different way. As with my car crash example, I would like you to start to see situations within your own experiences that could have a seed of benefit for you but as yet, until you look at it differently, the seed is still covered by the ground and only mud is currently obvious.

The Following are more examples from my references, where I have changed how I initially viewed the situation. I have altered them to provide me with an interpretation of the event that I can use to my positive advantage:

Weight Loss

I couldn't believe how fast weight can be lost due to the stress of separation. I am sure it is not recommended by Weight Watchers, but a more effective method would be hard to find. I lost 1½ stones in 3 months, however, I really liked it and I now endeavour to continue at this weight today. I did not consider myself overweight before but the benefits that the weight loss brought me were that I had no option but to buy some new clothes, I found that I felt fitter, more healthy, and I don't think it can hurt my chances when looking for a new partner!

Friends

I have mentioned along the way that I had a perception that I didn't have many close friends, especially in relation to 'everyone else'. I now know that I am truly blessed by friends. Friends who have stayed by me through this whole journey, friends that have always been there when I needed them or just to talk; God, I needed to talk! Friends who have given me encouragement, guidance, warmth and the freedom to be close or distant when needed.

Finance

My wife had always undertaken the administration of our finances. There were a number of areas I had no knowledge of and my initial thoughts were that it would take a lot of time and I could easily make mistakes. Now, for the first time, I am completely in control of my finances. I know where it goes, I have been able to change certain elements that I was unhappy with, and I put money aside to ensure that I can enjoy my time and opportunities.

- *List out recent events and see if you can find a different meaning for them, a more helpful 'interpretation' of a situation that will provide you with something that is useful to you, a more beneficial outcome than perhaps your current view on things.*
- *Ensure that your new interpretation feels right. Do not delude yourself. Ensuring that it fits with you, that it gives you energy, a lift or a buzz inside means that your interpretation is right according to your personal values and beliefs*

As with the explanation relating to our fears, this is another form of re-framing, that looks to alter the residual meaning we give to a situation that has occurred to us. Remember, the brain is naturally wired negatively. You will 'naturally' see an event in a negative way. The need here is to alter your take on life to reward yourself with positive, empowering reflections of events that occur. The event will still have happened but this change of approach will help you regain balance and control whilst assisting you to move forward.

Superior Relationships

> There comes a time when you 'know' that the relationship you had is over. Yet the ties between you, the 'invisible thread' that has bonded you together, will not break its hold. Strong emotions still have their grip around you but in the midst of it all the power of forgiveness is the ultimate release.

Journal Entry - 30th November

I cannot believe what I have done today! I have been having real issues with my thoughts about my wife, how I should be handling things and how to move on. During my walk I got angry and shouted that she is gone and I must move on.

This evening my wife came to the house for us to sort out the money. I did not feel very accommodating at first and I know it showed.

We then started a conversation and I said I found it hard to accept her talking about how other people were behaving when she was acting how she was. She then started crying when I said that all I saw was her hard stance. She said "how did I expect her to act?" and I said "as a real person".

I told her that a number of days before I had written in my journal that it would be a far bigger man than I currently am to ensure she was supported, but that is what I am offering. I said it was not based on wanting her back as she is adamant that she has made the right decision.

I said I thought she needed to concentrate her mind on what was good in her life even though this was tough at present.

I wanted to take the pressure away and help her with how she is communicating with herself and I said I would be supportive. I have no idea what this means for me. I really care for my wife.

I told her I knew she needed to do this to find out about herself, but she had taken the most dramatic route to do this. She said she still believed it was the right decision as she felt the relationship was going nowhere.

At this point in time I can only support my wife. I have to accept our split and carve out a new life for myself. At this time I have no idea how this will come about, with who or when.

Sometimes I think I am being 'holier than thou' and I told my wife I did not hate her as she thinks. I said I do not hate anyone as this does no good and just burns you away.

During this journey so far, we have reviewed many aspects of our relationships. There comes a time however when we need to take stock, when we need to take full responsibility and allow ourselves the opportunity to start moving in a different direction to let our future lives unfold.

But how do we break the 'invisible thread' that has bonded us together, a bond that has potentially been in place for many years?

You hear some people say that there was a day, they can probably name it, when they decided enough was enough. There was no going back, what they had between them had gone, in fact, the light bulb had just come on. For these people it appears that something specific happened to move them forward but, I believe, for the majority of us who have been told "I no longer love you the way I did" the reaching of this 'ending' point is a more gradual process.

The way we reach this point is not the issue. The issue is how to cut the thread, how to move on, how to let go, in fact how to start living again.

I have described how the brain builds up its skills through a process of repetition, doing the same thing over and over. Consider then the fact that you have been with this same person for many years. You were continually in each other's company, you built lives together that encompass children, homes, holidays, family and friends and you experienced an array of events and memories that have formed so strongly in your mind, defining part of who you are. We can now begin to understand how these neurological associations and huge emotional attachments create a bond between us that is like superglue; enormously strong, long lasting and extremely hard to break apart.

After the event of separation, you feel the destructive emotions of blame, fear and anger, emotions that have you gripped in a headlock so powerful that you can literally feel light headed. The blood flow feels constrained, restricting your ability to rationally think. Then, when you do think, the thoughts go around and around in your mind with no real possibility of solution. They become more and more complicated, confused and exhausting. You have metaphorically reached the gate called 'Open If You Dare'.

You now have the choice to reclaim your life and move forward, but where have you been? You have been in an emotional turmoil for many weeks, months or even years and now you are at a point of taking back the responsibility for your future.

Why has it taken you so long to reach this point? Why can't you just make a decision and move on? Why, when you shut your eyes at night, do you still see their face in front of you?

Obvious questions, considering your current situation. I believe the answer is in that magical term of 'accepting' them for what they are, just questions. When you look at the questions themselves they reveal why we have not been able to move on. For example, why has it taken so long to reach this point?

Who said there was a timetable allied to the speed of coming to this or any other decision? As we have seen, not one of us on this planet is the same, so who is determining the pace? We are run by time but time in this case is not relevant, we are where we are. I have had so many people say to me "You will look back in a year's time and see that it was all for the best". We know that what they say is designed to comfort us, but at the time they say it a year feels like an eternity, especially when you are struggling to even get through to the next day. Remember, the calendar time is irrelevant; it is how you come through the other side that is important.

When you retain feelings, such as hate, despair, blame or anger, against your previous partner you are still linked through that 'invisible thread'. Your negative, emotional conversations with them, either in person or within your mind, is still linking you to them. The intertwining of your thoughts curtails your ability to move forward.

You may think that feeling the connection to these negative emotions will provide you with the degree of leverage you need to cut this 'invisible thread'. I am here to tell you that this is not the way. Just visualise for a moment the person you feel hate and anger for. Tell me, do they feel closer to you or further away? You are there with them still, are you not? You are there; bonded by the things you want to escape from, because you are using the wrong emotions to break free.

Someone I met recently, whose relationship had broken down, described to me her shock following a conversation she had with a work colleague. This colleague, who had gone through a divorce a number of years earlier, was considered by the other people in the office to be very reserved, polite and balanced. The shock came when, with quiet ferocity, the colleague proceeded to impart her strategy for getting what she wanted from her estranged husband: "Now remember, you have the kids, if he doesn't pay or do what you want then he doesn't get to see the children, you have the power!".

Where can this line of thinking take you? Can you imagine using children as pawns in a chess game of emotion, trading money or things for love? How deep the scars on all concerned when the level of anger, mistrust, hurt and pain reach this level of acuteness.

My advice is to be easy on yourself. Think, picture and feel this; imagine that you are walking against a very strong wind. How does it feel? It is hard work, you are struggling just to stand upright, the intense power of the wind against your body quickly drains your energy. After a very short period of time your resistance is exhausted and you want to turn around and go home. The effort is wearing you out and you just want to go back to where you were.

Think and picture now that the force of the wind is behind you. You now experience a magical difference. You feel as if you are literally being swept along, no effort involved in easily moving forward, you could go for miles as the energy taken to move across the ground is minimal.

What feels easy is the right course. If something feels a struggle, draining of energy or patently wrong inside of you, then you should seriously question if it is the right thing to do. The right thing to do might involve hard work. If you are doing something in a different way, because of what you have learnt here or elsewhere, it will take energy and persistence, but if it feels the right thing to do then the effort will be worthwhile. Use your feelings to help you navigate. This will ensure that you are going in the right direction, that you are doing the right thing.

Take very small, easy steps and you will get there, I promise you. Do not take notice of time. Do take into consideration what others say, then take notice of what, for you, feels easy and what feels right. This is the way.

It is difficult to approach a situation, such as conflict, using different methods and emotions to those you instinctively utilise. It goes against most of what we have been taught, and when you have been hurt by another it is seemingly natural to react with retribution, revenge or a whole myriad of other negative responses.

We should not ignore however, how negative emotions can be used to positively affect your motivation to start doing something. Anger, for instance, can be a great tool to move you from procrastination into action. You can use this emotion to push you into doing something, no matter how small, which has the subsequent effect of releasing you from the shackles of your mind.

The art of using an emotion like anger, or any other negative response, is to ensure that it is short lived. Use the burst of anger to release you and then let it go. Retaining anger against something or someone burns a hole within your insides that can literally kill you. This is not written for effect. Think of people who you have come across in your life who are angry; how do they look, how do they sound, how healthy is their skin, how healthy are their relationships?

The most powerful of the alternative responses I have found is to forgive the person for what they have done. My goodness, I can almost feel the reactions to this option. How can you forgive someone who has caused you so much pain? How can you forgive someone who has destroyed what you thought was your future? How can you forgive this person who once told you they loved you and now they do not, or at least do not in the same way?

There is an old saying 'forgive and forget'. I do not advocate in one way or another whether you must forget this person (you cannot anyway for they are part of your history). The principle here is to release yourself towards your new future.

Once you decide to forgive the other person you immediately reclaim the three principles that I have spoken of in other sections, namely Your Power, Your Direction, and Your Ability to Act. You now have control.

Remember how I described what it felt like to be powerless, rudderless and waiting? If you have accepted where you are, if you now understand how damaging the retaining of powerful negative emotions can be, upon your energies, your health and your ability to interpret situations, you have reached the point where you can dramatically start to move forward by forgiving the other person for what they have done.

Does forgiveness mean that you fully understand and accept what the other person has done? I still do not fully understand the reasons behind my wife's actions, and I probably never will. The point of forgiveness is to allow YOU the opportunity to move forward, to enable YOU to re-take control of your life, in fact this action of forgiveness is for YOU, it is not about how this affects the other person.

Does forgiveness mean you are being weak? I am not advocating a capitulation on what you deserve to retrieve from the partnership, be this financial or otherwise. In fact, think about it. You will be putting into practice a method rarely used by people to overcome this trauma; you will be flowing with rather than going against the normal tide of negatively driven reactions. I would suggest that this 'forgiveness' displays strength of character far ahead of the

Martin J. Whelan

other person, who unfortunately is dealing with this situation without knowing that there are alternative responses.

Does forgiveness mean that they were right and you were wrong? Every one of us will see the same event differently. If you could cut inside your partner's brain and hear what torment was going through their minds I believe that you would quickly realise that they are suffering too.

Does forgiveness mean that you have to tell the other person? I would suggest that this thought is for you alone. This action is for you, and you do not have to try to explain it to anyone else. Can you imagine trying to justify, either to your partner, or to a friend or relative, why you have taken this action? Imagine having to justify the word 'forgive' to them without their knowledge of what you have read and all the things you have been working on to this point. No, keep this inside of you for your own nourishment, your own growth.

The time of the tennis match is over. Thoughts of blame, anger, hate or revenge are written deeply into the fabric of that ball going back and forward over the net. I want you now to smash that ball out of the stadium. Envisage yourself reclaiming your power of decision to forgive your partner for what they have done, envisage reclaiming the direction of your life in line with your dream and the realisation that you have the ability to **act**. Forgive and move on.

Exercise 19 - The Power Of Forgiving

You will probably feel sick in the first instance doing this exercise, as you will be saying things to yourself that are potentially diametrically opposed to all the things you have thought up to this point.

One part of my dream is that I want to ensure that I retain a good relationship with my wife. She is the mother of my children. We spent many happy years together. We have many good memories. Why should I wish to destroy these positive thoughts because our marriage is no more? Why leave a trail of destruction where many good things have happened? Forgive and move on.

- *I want you to detail how you are now going to allow yourself to move forward by forgiving your partner for what they have done.*
- *I also want you to re-visit your dream. Is it strong enough? Can you really feel it? Were there elements of the dream still linked to your partner?*

One of the ultimate challenges to the human being is to forgive someone for causing such intense grief and pain. Strongly linked to acceptance and interpretation, the power gained by the individual of forgiving someone is extensively expressed in Buddhist practices.

Get Back Out There

Many couples become totally intertwined during the course of
their relationship, sharing all aspects of life. After a separation
occurs the individual needs to re-discover their social
independence, but how? You just bite the bullet, get out there
and dance the night away.

Journal Entry - 4th November

My dance class yesterday was really enjoyable; I won a prize,
was asked to be team leader and enjoyed meeting all the new
people.

The lady of my dreams was not there although I was
attracted to an Austrian woman who was 45-50 I think, had
a great figure and was elegant. She was with her man but we
spoke about Austria and Vienna and I could tell she enjoyed
this.

Today Tony called me and we spoke for an hour. He said
I had done a lot of good work. I know I will have difficult
times but at present I feel robust, relatively in control of
my mental state and am living on a day to day basis whilst
looking forward.

In some ways I am happy. Happy that I can release
through the dancing, happy that I am starting to see the

fog clear, happy that the effects of this event are not leaving me with negatives but with more love for others than ever before. I feel I just want to share things with other people, enable them to have a great life and to bring joy into their worlds. I hope I am not locked up soon!!!

The reading of the 'Monk book' [see below] has had a major effect on me at this time. The listing of my fears has been revealing as I know these have been with me for many years. I am sure that when I have dealt with these more will surface but I know these are at the core of releasing my future life.

Reading the book today one bit struck me; right at the beginning when Dar first met Julian he said that he had 'never met anyone who exuded such power'. The reason this struck a chord is that a couple of weeks ago I felt this power in me but from a negative perspective. This is what I want to project but from a positive, loving perspective. This will come.

I am out tonight with Graeme who I met through the car crash. I have no idea how this will go but I know this is behind my thoughts of meeting a person near to where I live who is in a similar situation to me.

A major issue following a relationship split is the reclaiming of self from a social perspective. Again, I can only speak for myself in this context as I know many people continue to follow individual interests when they are in a relationship. For me, in the main, my social life revolved around my wife and I. Our social circle mainly consisted of quiz nights, annual celebrations, meals out and family gatherings.

Following the separation, I had to consider how I was going to get back into the world of singletons. As detailed previously, I am not a pub man or heavy drinker, but I found myself having to push myself to make such arrangements to re-establish a social network. I had to get out of the house and start to explore what being a single man of 48 would be like out there.

Three months after the event I plucked up the courage to venture into the world of dance. For a number of years friends of mine had been doing a dance called Ceroc, a form of salsa and jive, which I thoroughly enjoyed but found hugely frustrating to learn.

Ceroc gave me many things. Consider the situation; where else on a Tuesday evening would I get to meet more than 30 ladies, dance with them, speak to them, laugh with them (if you saw my dancing in the early days you would know why we were laughing) and enjoy one of my greatest loves, music? It was through Ceroc that I met my first girlfriend after my separation and I will never forget that amazing experience.

Many times at Ceroc I would wonder about the reasons other people had for being there. Perhaps, like me, the opportunity to meet someone, to get fit, to enjoy the music, express themselves, learn something new, or feel part of a community. Whatever the reasons, I was glad they were there.

For me, Ceroc gave me a purpose, it gave me hope and it gave me a refuge where I could be anonymous with no pressures to tell anyone anything about me. I could escape into a different world for two hours, unable to think of anything else other than learning to dance. All of the issues I had in my life were put on hold, my mind diverted, my thoughts channelled into a pleasurable activity.

I cannot forget however the massive stress and mental chatter I had to deal with before attending my first class. Working in the sales industry for many years has given me the confidence to walk through many doors, but that first night of Ceroc is still so vivid in my mind.

On that first night, walking through that door was such a difficult thing for me to do. I did not know anyone, I did not know how to do the dance, I did not know how things worked, I did not know where to stand, in fact, why the hell had I put myself in this position?

I paid my joining fee, purchased a drink and then nervously waited for the first part of the evening to begin. After a few warm up exercises the dance teacher duly instructed us to take hold of our partners and pull them in close. I had been ordered to hold a woman in my arms after months of dreaming of nothing else! Control was needed but I felt I had none. It was just like the first day of school when everything is new and you are the proverbial 'King who had lost his clothes'. I felt stripped bare of all I knew, exposed to completely different stimuli and exposed like a little child stuck in the middle of the playground.

You know what, though? The people were great. They were really pleased to welcome new dancers and they had a beginner's class just for people like me. A beautiful thing I found, very subtle but very powerful, was that a rule of Ceroc is that you cannot refuse someone a dance. How releasing for the ego when you know that whoever you ask to take to the floor will say yes. Brilliant, especially when I remember the fragile state I was in at first.

Over the course of a few dance classes a number of very interesting phenomena became apparent to me:

- Doing something new or different can actually become more difficult after the first or second time. When your experience is fresh and the components are still unknown the mind has not had a chance to build up any habits, norms or patterns to the new activity. It has not had the chance to start referencing the past or projecting the future, so the little 'fear' stories that formulate inside of us haven't had the opportunity yet to be written.

I found after three weeks I started to have difficulty attending the venue. My mind began to construct fears or at best limiting thoughts. I pondered that I would 'know' who would be there, some people who you liked, some not so much. My expectations and subsequent pressure on myself grew as I perceived that by now, I should be able to do the moves. All of these things were being manufactured inside my head as no one had said anything. I had not been made to stand in the corner because of not doing a move properly, people still smiled as they moved from dancer to dancer. Perhaps my ego was starting to get in the way again?

- Men are, in the main, solitary animals, especially in this type of environment. I am a chatterer and love to talk, but I noticed a distinct lack of other men wanting to engage in much conversation. You could say I had my priorities in the wrong place and I should be chatting to the ladies, which I certainly did, but this trend about the man was very obvious. It reminded me of a kind of peacock strutting dance exhibition where they were out to prove that they were the top male catch. I just wonder if this is how the ladies see it?

- I reflected on the thought that before this event happened in my life, I had often sat at home thinking of attending a dance class. I now knew that people were, at that very moment, experiencing exactly what I was thinking about. All of that energy, enjoyment, laughter and chemistry being released in a hall 12 miles from my home and I was sat there watching TV. I reflected that there is life out there; I just needed to go and grab it!

Exercise 20 - It's All Going On Out There!

You are rebuilding your life. As difficult as it may seem, you are fully responsible for how your future will develop. Now is the time to ensure that you are doing things that fire you up, stimulate you and make you feel alive.

- *How has your social calendar been affected by the separation?*
- *How do you feel you will be able to grow your social network?*
- *What things in the past have you often thought you would love to try but have never taken the opportunity to, or perhaps have been dissuaded by your partner from doing? This could be dancing, yoga, guitar lessons, a pottery class (I know you have that 'Ghost' film memory in your mind!), swimming.*
- *Ideally, choose something that is regular, for instance weekly, something for you to look forward to again in only a few days time.*
- *Add this social chapter to your dream*

A common sense lesson involving the philosophy 'you are responsible for your world'. The ability to start to play again with life, to try new things that stimulate and refresh you as an individual, moves you from the status of 'victim' to being the creator of your future.

Writers Note:

Since my relationship split, I have continued to read many books, of which two in particular have been instrumental in helping me through this time. They have enabled me to understand the emotions I had been feeling, to understand why the event had such an impact on me and, just as importantly, they have given me a framework to use for my recovery.

The 'Monk Book' described in the last journal entry is 'Discover Your Destiny with The Monk Who Sold His Ferrari, Through the Seven Stages of Self Awakening': Robin Sharma has created an elegant story providing the reader with an explanation of a journey we undertake if we want to reclaim our true self. A self that is independent, giving, loving and free to choose the best path forward.

The other book which has become a cornerstone of my route back to myself is 'Intimacy' by Osho. This is a very deep view of the human psychology, and looks at how we can change our perspectives on subjects that can impact upon our relationships. A profound lesson contained within the pages helped me with overcoming my situation regarding Loneliness. He described that, until you are able to deal with what he called 'aloneness' and become independent without fear, you can never truly be free to love another.

Trust

> *When trust is shattered by a relationship split a natural response is to safeguard oneself, to hold people at arm's length, to put a distance between you and future possible pain. The solution is crazy but true. You have to trust more than ever before and that trust all starts with you!*

Journal Entry - 11th November

I am writing this sat on the ferry to Ireland. It always amazes me that with the relative ease of travel today we can wake up in our home and a few hours later be departing for another country.

It feels very strange travelling on my own. It is not an issue but I am so used to sharing my journeys with others, especially my wife, I seem in another world.

I have decided to be upbeat for the whole week in Ireland. I will be with people all the time, I will be paid for the majority of the trip, I am getting used to being *martinwhelan.com*, and I could die on this ship! As unlikely as this is it could happen and then what would all my anguish have been for?

I really know that my wife and I are finished. During my drive down to the ferry I reflected on how we had been together in the recent past, what the potential for going forward would be and I come to a blank position. The key thing now is to focus on my future.

I am very clear about what I want in the future. I do have concerns of course, namely, when will it happen, how will it happen, why should it happen to me? I have always struggled with not working everything out and trusting things out of my control. However I know I need to let this happen and trust that what I dream will become a reality. It is no good purporting my 'learning' without walking my talk.

Looking around the ship at people I wonder what is in their minds. Most of them will not have any knowledge about the paradigms of life and I wonder if it is a good thing or bad thing that there are differences? I do not see, other than small children, people bursting with life and energy, and it is clear that we do not make the most of every day, me definitely included. It feels inappropriate to be very different but I will communicate with as many people as possible, both verbal and non verbal, to do my bit to lift the average of how we as people go through the day, and possibly our whole lives.

"Train yourself to let go of everything you fear to lose", a quote from Master Yoda. Look back at these words again, a profound statement entwined within the production of a Hollywood block buster.

What does it mean 'Train yourself to let go of everything you fear to lose'?

We have looked at how our fears can seriously hold us back from living the life we truly dream about. Now this philosophy states that we have to be prepared to let go of everything that we 'own'. This perception of 'ownership' causes us to try to hang onto it, to safeguard our 'property' at all costs and not do anything that may disturb the equilibrium of our current situation.

After a relationship split you feel that you have indeed 'lost everything we fear to lose'. You have lost what you had built on an intimate level and lost what can best be described as 'things'.

'Things' are items such as houses, furniture, cars, clothes, holidays, dining out, friends, the garden, music concerts, family ties. All of the 'visible' pieces of the jigsaw that were components of the life that you shared with someone else, parts of your life that had become the norm of what you had come to know yourself by, they were a reflection of you.

On an intimate level, it is the loss of a depth of contact which became your known way of being on a daily basis. You perhaps had an understanding, both verbal and unsaid, where you could literally read each other's minds. You would know how the other would react to certain situations, where the cross over points were, and when a change in stance and tact would be required. You had a matching of intellect and mental 'tuning' that enabled you to communicate together freely, easily and topically. You had an overall feeling of connection on an emotional level that provided a foundation to the way you went about your day. Now, through this relationship split all these have gone.

So, how can you learn to trust again? Descriptive words for the term trust are: faith, belief, conviction, confidence, expectation, reliance, dependence, hope. When I review this array of words I can only come to the conclusion that trust, and all it encompasses, is one of the most fundamental elements integral to our relationships.

You need faith that the other will always be there for you, either physically or emotionally. You need a belief that someone truly loves you for who you are, that they have the same conviction to build a life together and a confidence that you are both heading in the same direction. You need a glow of expectation that your goals and dreams can be realised together, that you are able to be reliant upon the other to provide strength in areas that you feel weak in, you can depend on their contribution to the home and finances and a hope that you will always be together.

Through our relationship breakdown, the principle of trust is shattered. The invisible blanket that surrounded you both is no more. There is an enforced change to your fundamental beliefs and a situation you previously considered 'right', or the way things were meant to be, has vanished.

So, how to trust again? You have to. I am here to tell you that if you wish to have a fully developed relationship in the future you have to trust; and the person you first have to trust is you!

When the trust between people is broken, especially where intimacy has been experienced and enjoyed, it is a very human trait to generalise and feel that there is no one who you can truly believe in.

I would like you to consider the following; what can you judge to really be true and genuine as, in essence, when someone is being 'true and genuine' it is based upon their own picture, their own feelings and their own interpretation of these words?

For example; someone might not tell you about a situation because they fear that you would be upset if you knew. They did not want to increase your unhappiness so they display 'true and genuine' friendship to you by not telling you. You on the other hand wanted to know the 'whole' truth, but again this is a truth from your perspective. A complicated arena, as I am sure you can start to see.

I believe that most people view themselves as trustworthy; that their actions, as in this example, were based upon what they thought and felt to be the right ones to take at that time.

This whole scenario leads me to conclude that the only true path is to trust in you completely. A trust constructed according to your personal set of beliefs, hopes and truths.

Through the exercises that you have participated in, you will have built a blueprint of what is truly important to you. You will have developed a model of how you will operate moving forward and you will know what you will and as importantly, what you will not tolerate in your life.

You have to develop an inner strength of trust that enables you to make your decisions based upon what feels correct for you. No longer will you be dependent on or at the mercy of others. Trust in yourself will ensure that no one has the ability to take the foundations of trust away from you, never again will anyone be able to destroy your faith, belief, conviction, confidence, expectation, reliance, dependence and hope.

I want you to complete the next exercise related to trust whilst utilising the art of listening to what you are hearing and feeling inside. You have a massive directional guidance system inside of you that is widely ignored, or at least not understood by the majority of us.

I once saw a documentary about the American business tycoon Donald Trump who was asked by the interviewer how he makes his business decisions. Thinking that this might be very useful in the world of making my fortune I ran and got a piece of paper and drew the chair slightly closer to the TV (no idea why when I could turn the sound up but that's just me I guess). Mr Trump then proceeded to inform us of his strategy: "I get my aides to look at all of the detail available, produce future profit projections for opportunity growth and create for me the most effective way to raise the capital for the venture. They bring it to me, I then review all of the evidence in front of me and" - at this point my pen is poised, ready to write down the key reason why this man has become a multi billionaire - "then I put it in my gut to give me the answer. Even if all of the evidence says everything is brilliant about the deal, if the gut says no then it goes no further, I trust my instincts to guide me". Millions of dollars worth of decision based upon your insides, can this be true?

When something is right or wrong for you then you will feel this inside if you listen to it. To warm you up for this exercise, think now of a very special, fantastic, emotional moment in your life and notice where in your body the great feeling occurs. For me I get this in the pit of my stomach with a warm glow emanating up my centre.

Now think of something bad that has happened to you and notice where you get this feeling. For me it is in my chest and gives me a queasy feeling in my stomach. Now you have your internal directional guidance system that is free to be used by you 24 hours a day.

Start now to develop your personal portrait of the components that are really important to you on the subject of trust. Use yourself as your guide to what is correct for you for your future. Create a portfolio of inner strength which cannot be taken away by anyone else.

When you "Train yourself to let go of everything you fear to lose", remember the way that we enter into the world. We are naked, we know nothing. We are not concerned about the style of our house or the type of shoes we are wearing, the size of our bank balance or our partner. We are in fact, totally free.

The more we fear losing those 'things' that we build into our lives the more likely it is that we will indeed lose them. Try holding onto water and what does it do? It slips through your hands. Try catching the wind that blows your hair and you will not be able to find anything there, however, without water, without air, we are no more, within these fundamentals life truly is.

By trusting yourself, by "Training yourself to let go of everything you fear to lose", you will find that your ability to trust others will increase dramatically as you are not dependent upon them or 'things'; you are free to decide.

Exercise 21 - Trust in Yourself

I want to encourage you with this exercise to look at the fundamentals for your life, the bedrock that your existence is based upon, and trust what this tells you.

- *Can you identify times where you have not trusted your instincts?*
- *What have been the results?*
- *When everything is stripped away, who are you?*
- *What do you truly believe in?*
- *What do you stand for?*
- *What will you never tolerate in your life again?*
- *What makes you intensely happy?*
- *Add whatever surfaces through this exercise to your dream*

According to the teachings of the Tao, we never truly own a thing, possession or person. We are essentially custodians for a period of time, a time that is undefined in duration. Severe anguish is felt when we consume ourselves in the protection of what we fear to loose from our lives. This protection results in the loss of joy surrounding the 'thing' that we were so desperate to keep. Trust and let your instincts and life be your guide whilst fully enjoying what you have today.

Rules

> *Our entry back into the world of relationships can appear a scary place, where pain and hurt exist amongst love and connection. A method of protection, defined as 'rules' can look to be the way to defending oneself against the possibility of further anguish. It appears however that 'rules' really are there to be broken.*

"Deflector Shields up, Mr Sulu, we are heading for enemy territory."

The definition of a Deflector Shield on the official Star Trek web site states: *'A type of force field that surrounds a starship, space station or planet to protect against enemy attack or natural hazard.'*

When we enter back into the world of relationships, we have to expose ourselves again to an environment where we know emotions such as pain, hurt, anxiety and fear lurk alongside the beautiful feelings of togetherness, trust, comfort, love, support and sharing.

As a means of protection, many people re-enter the world of relationships braced with a set of definitions and conditions that, I believe, massively affect the quality of their future interpersonal lives; 'I will never live with anyone again', 'I want to see someone just at weekends', 'I have no problem if they see other people', 'once bitten twice shy', 'easy come easy go', 'I want no commitments', 'no one will ever hurt me like that again'.

These are but a few examples of phrases that, once adopted into our belief systems, start, whether consciously or unconsciously, to produce the desired outcome. These people are creating a set of working operandi which I define as 'rules'; Rules to block past pain, rules to ensure that nobody can get close enough to leave the trail of damage that has been experienced before, rules that essentially set the platform for the next relationship.

As with the exercise relating to trust, we need to determine where the thresholds are. For instance, if there was a level of mental or physical abuse in your last relationship it would be a valuable rule to establish that this is something you will not tolerate from your new partner. Another totally reasonable rule would be that you will not tolerate a relationship where an addiction to drink or drugs is evident. A reasonable rule would be that all parties work for a living without reliance on social benefits. A basic rule I have is that my partner has to accept my son and my dog as part of me, the package.

These types of rules I am totally in favour of, where you determine the basic standards or values of how you want to live.

The type of rules I am challenging here are where you lay down a doctrine of how, in essence, you try to control your future possibilities based either upon a type of prejudice or on past experiences; the person has to be short, they have to be tall, they have to have a nice car, they have to be from a good background, they have to have plenty of money, they have to have a degree, they must be younger / older / the same age as me, they must be a Taurus, they must be able to ski, they have to be good in bed.

Link this sample of rules with the protective sayings or definitions that are used to ensure that hurt is not possible in the future, and we arrive at the metaphoric purchase of a blue shirt, tie and cufflinks.

Based upon previous history, you have decided to buy a blue shirt, tie and cufflinks in a box set, as it will be easier and quicker to purchase and, most importantly, you know what you are getting! Inside the box we have the blue shirt. Now, the shade of blue isn't exactly what you wanted, but it will do. The tie is a bit too flowery to go with the striping within the suit but, hey, the tie will not be worn for long. The cufflinks are a bit sparkly for your liking but that's ok, the jacket can be kept on all evening.

All of this compromise because you set out to the shops with a set of rules that said you had to buy a box set of blue shirt, tie and cufflinks. A strategy you thought would make your life safer and more straightforward, whilst also not having to select what you wanted on individual merit.

Please do not misunderstand me. I know that we all have preferences. There are certain types of people we are attracted to, the colour of their hair, or no hair, the shape of their eyes, the way they carry themselves, how they laugh or their level of conversation. What I am encouraging here is for you to have an openness which will allow you as many possibilities as you can for that new, right person to enter into your life.

Take the box set example: When you walk into a shop and you are just looking for box sets your options are immediately limited. You find that there are only seven different sets available in total, and only three with blue shirts! What happens however when you consider the items individually? You now have hundreds of combinations to tempt you, all of the shirts in the blue section, fabulous racks of ties and a complete display cabinet full of cufflinks. Now you are open to possibility.

You have a basic idea of what you are looking for, as you have defined the fundamental components you must have, but now you are free to open your mind to other options. You are open to other colours, open to other combinations that may now feel right because you are looking at what you want without an array of limiting rules to curtail your opportunities.

When considering the Star Trek example it is interesting to note that they only raised the shields when they detected danger. Why not leave them up all the time and then they would always be protected? I would suggest that the ship's deflector shields use up a great amount of energy if they are continually deployed. Also, by looking only through the shield for enemies, the crew would have seriously limited their capability to see and discover other fantastic planets within the solar systems. But, perhaps most importantly, they realised that the vast majority of people out there are friendly, are considerate, are warm and are looking for the same thing as you; why then continually protect oneself because of the few?

Exercise 22 - Rules Are Made To Be Broken

The rules for my future relationship are, I believe, very simple; my new lady loves me as much as I do her and she accepts Gary and Harvey as part of me as I accept her family as part of her. With this basic level of defined 'rules' my window of opportunity, I believe, is vast! All of my other 'desires', my other 'wishes' are encompassed within my dream. The rules for my relationship could not be simpler.

- *What 'rules' have you secretly, or not so secretly, set up regarding your next relationship? List them down.*
- *Having now viewed my perspective on rules, identify which ones are fundamentals, which are not negotiable.*

Another way to understand what are fundamentals is to utilise the phrase 'what must you have' from your next partner.

- *Now identify which ones come into the category of the box set, too defining and restricting. Review this second set and remodel them to dramatically open up your options for moving forward.*
- *List out your defined rules*
- *Add your 'desires' and 'wishes' to your dream*

Rules lie deep within the subconscious. Fundamentally, they are part of our belief system. To alter rules we have to bring our thoughts into our conscious mind, review them and then determine whether they are useful to us or not. As with any other change of belief, the adjustment will require effort, patience and practice. Dramatically reducing our rules, or self imposed restrictions or limitations, exponentially opens up a new world of possibilities to enter into our lives.

Open Your Arms

What have you now to fear? You have reflected and taken action on so many aspects of your previous view of the world that you are now in a completely different place. If you have accepted the challenges of this journey back to yourself, your new partner will be embraced like never before.

Picture now that you have started a new romance and you are in a discussion with your new partner. Because you have both established limiting rules for your future relationship and you have both been damaged along the way, you realise that the level of commitment that will exist between you will be limited. How do you feel about not being fully open with each other? Through this discussion, you now realise that the level of trust will be kept at a moderate standard, the degree of intimacy between you may be superficial, the being together will be partially fulfilling and adequate; in summary, this will be an ok relationship. How do you feel?

If you have participated in the exercises within this book, you will have recalled the trauma you felt when your partner took their love away. You were left empty and cold as you were in effect dependent upon your partner for your security. Now, through your efforts, you have re-defined that you as an individual are totally capable of supporting yourself. You have accepted the situation, moved on and you have chosen not to become entwined in the bitterness of blame, hate and anger. You have determined what you want in your world and are secure in the knowledge that, although being single it is not the way you always want to live your life, you now know how to survive and prosper on your own.

I propose that you look to enter into your new relationship **more open than at any time before**!

Remember, you now have very firm foundations; you are in control and are not at the mercy of another's ability to manipulate you. So now, possibly for the first time, you can truly engage with another!

When we think about our new partner and our thoughts sound something like; 'I need to be in this relationship because I am so lonely and I require their love and affection', we are communicating a void in our life, a having to have, a need of a supportive relationship because we lack something within ourselves.

Consider the different emotions that surface with a thought such as 'I love being in this relationship as I want us to really enjoy each other's company every day'. Here we have created a feeling and a picture in our minds of openness, simplicity and mutual respect. This style of thought demonstrates that we are strong, we are self sufficient, and above all we are open; open to fully explore the magic of the relationship based upon love, affection, sharing and being.

I encourage you to hold back not one thing! If it feels right commit fully to the relationship as if it will last forever. Be totally open, be yourself, truly be with the other person. Do you know what will happen if you do this? The other person will think and feel that you are extraordinary. Very few people are fully open in their relationships; most keep a parachute in reserve 'just in case'. You have taken this opportunity to define what would be right and what would be wrong in your life, so now you will know, from the very start, if this relationship is right for you. One piece of warning; this will be so as long as you stay true to yourself.

It is said that 'our sorrow is our joy disguised.' For me this means that when we feel so dreadful about something that has happened, it is because what that something gave us was where we found our happiness. If we do not enter the world where sorrow lurks then we will never again find our joy.

You know something? Pain may come again. Things are not going to always work out how you wish them to. You may find that someone else causes you pain, perhaps in a different way than you have previously experienced, but what will you also know? You will know that you were totally open. You will know you gave your all. You will know you fully enjoyed things whilst the relationship lasted. You will know that you were free from the shackles of your previous experiences and, that you lived life to the full.

Exercise 23 - Living Totally

Don't hold back because of 'what might' happen. The time honoured saying "We get what we think about, whether we like it or not" asks us to consider that the way we communicate to ourselves within our minds brings about its physical manifestation. If you think the relationship will work or the relationship won't work you are right! You are communicating a thought that will transpire in the future. Be very conscious of what and how you think!

- *Have you again, consciously or unconsciously, built up a barrier to your new relationship, never wanting to feel that level of pain again?*
- *Describe the things you have been saying to yourself, can you now understand where they are taking you?*

- *Have you had other relationships and found that you have held yourself back? What were the consequences?*
- *Are you now able to allow yourself to fully commit to your next relationship?*
- *Have you done the foundational work that will allow you to really go into your next chapter with a totally open heart?*

An area of great importance within the practice of Neuro Linguistic Programming is to understand the syntax used by the patient. Syntax means the order and sequence of the words that are used, either audible to others or, just as importantly, internal within their own dialogue. By altering the syntax we alter the feelings that are generated towards a more manageable level of emotion. We are lightening the power of the statement expressed and transform it to produce the desired result as opposed to an unwanted fear.

Who Am I Now?

Who is this person staring back at you in the mirror? What have you learnt during this journey back to yourself? Have you come to terms with the fact that what others see is not the real you, that actually what 'is' you is on the inside? How far have you come?

So, who am I now? Well, my name is Martin, I am 48 years old, I live in Oxfordshire in the UK, I drive a BMW, I was married for 26 years, I have a son Gary who is 24, my parents live in Buckinghamshire, I have had an interesting career so far, I am now writing a book.

When we were at school we were often asked to describe ourselves (probably to enable the teachers to try to understand what the hell they had in front of them!) and my format was always like the last paragraph, but really, who am I?

Who am I when all of the labels are taken away, when the definition of my age does not mean that I am old or I am young, it simply means that I have spent a period of time on this earth, classified by 365 days equating to 1 year?

If you have been completing the exercises in this book you will have started to see a picture emerge about yourself. A picture of how your 'type' of thinking was hindering your progress, a picture of how the way you were seeing your situation may have limited your options for a fantastic future life.

When defined by our labels, we are essentially looking at the external vision of us as an individual. When we walk down the street we look at other people and start to do what I call categorise: "They are well off; they are struggling for money; how skinny is she?; who ate all the pies?; they have beautiful hair; they need a haircut; my God I am so attracted to her; never in a month of Sundays would I want to be with them".

All of these judgements made just by walking down the street. Judgements created inside of us through observing, categorising and selecting, according to our own personal preferences.

We experience this obsession with 'labels' strongly every day through the 'information' provided by the media. Every article about a celebrity seemingly mentions their wealth, their main attribute, for example Jennifer Anniston and her hair, their age and who they were last married to, engaged to, going out with.

So is this what we are, a collection of labels like money being pinned onto a bride and groom at a Greek wedding? This surely must be what we work all of our lives to achieve; status, recognition, financial security, position and respect. This must be the purpose in life; to gain all of these 'things' in order to demonstrate to others how far we have come from the cradle, display what we have made of ourselves and show how we stand ahead of others in the queue.

When I started to strip away the external labels I judged myself against, I became really unsure about 'who' I had become. Who was this person looking back at me in the mirror? I had assembled a number of prizes along the way and worked really hard to get them. The quest for gold however was always there. After gaining a piece I would then set off on another escapade in order for me to really find my destiny, really find my true position in life and allow me to demonstrate to others that I was worthy of the labels I placed upon my suit.

The breakup of my marriage literally stopped me in my tracks. Had I really been enjoying life, feeling fantastic about each new day, breathing in new air that would allow me to get that next great prize? No, I was bloody knackered. This continual fight with life had brought this situation to a head, something had to change.

I began to think about people I really admired. My Grandmother was a great inspiration for anyone who came into her presence. When I attended her funeral I could not believe the number of mourners who attended, 1,000 people would not be an underestimate. I use the word 'mourners', but I really should use the word 'celebrators', as this is how it felt. This huge array of people attended my Grandmother's funeral to celebrate her life of 91 years.

So what level of fame and career did my Grandmother have in her lifetime? She had lived in the same small town in the south of Ireland all her life, she had no real formal education and after my Grandfather died at an early age she brought up a family of 13 children in a 'two up two down' cottage. Her furthest foreign travel was to the UK to visit some of her children who had moved there and she loved to sing, dance and play the accordion.

So what made 1,000 people attend her funeral that day? What pulling power did she have? What made those people want to show respect to my Grandmother's life, as she certainly didn't have any 'labels' on her clothes, no traditional signs of having 'made it'?

In an amazingly humble way, she had affected a huge number of people around her. She had helped others in the town and surrounding villages literally from the cradle to the grave. Remember, we are talking of a period of time when people were essentially fending for their own survival; a health service, especially in Ireland at this time, was virtually non-existent.

At one end of the spectrum my Grandmother delivered a huge number of the local children, and in traditional Irish fashion, these were plentiful. At the other end of their journey she laid people out to rest when they had passed away. I can recall her telling us stories of people where, after their heart had stopped, they could pass wind from either end of their bodies and that some corpses would even be known to sit up when rigor mortis set in! No wonder as children we were enthralled, but never wanted to go to sleep after hearing some of her recollections.

She performed all of these local duties whilst bringing up a family of 13. She shared everything she had with those who were less fortunate. She never placed herself above, or below, anyone else and she ensured that she rejoiced in the pleasures of life through music and laughter. I can now fully understand why 1,000 people attended her funeral.

I believe people respected my Grandmother because she knew who she was inside; she was warm, strong, caring and very astute but, above all, she gave love in everything she did.

Shortly after my marriage separation I went to Ireland to visit my family. Being only a few months into coming to terms with what had happened to me I was deeply troubled and had serious questions spinning around in my mind. I decided to visit my Grandmother's grave and ask her the key question that was plaguing me at the time. I had not been to the graveyard since her burial a number of years before and could not find her grave, so I decided, after searching for half an hour, to simply walk in the graveyard and ask the question.

Immediately an answer shot into my head that I know could only have been from my Grandmother, as it had the directness and steely perception innate within her. She told me "you have to decide!" I had been asking her a specific question, and I wanted her to take the responsibility from me by telling me what to do. Never in a million years would she have taken that responsibility from anyone; she definitely would have had an opinion on the subject, but she knew instinctively that the only person who could make that level of decision was me.

Now was this all in my mind or had I been communicated with from another world? I suggest it doesn't matter, as my purpose in recalling this story is to open up your thoughts to the fact that it is who we are inside rather than what we have that defines us as human beings. It is not the number of Gucci bags or the type of BMW car we drive that provides our standing in this world, it is the quality of individual we are that sets us apart.

In my opinion there is absolutely nothing wrong in desiring to own nice things, striving to achieve goals, pushing the boundaries of what you think you can do whilst creating a fantastic environment and legacy for you and the people you love around you. I feel these challenges give us energy on a daily basis; they give us a reason to get out of bed in the morning with a belief that we are creating a path for our future, all tied together by a dream of where we are heading. Yes, your dreams are so important, but I want to remind you of some basic principles that I only came to realise after my event:

> Please do not become defined by the things that you have, believing that these are what you stand for and what you will protect at all costs. Unfortunately, when we fear the loss of something we start to bring this possibility into existence, and we also lose the beauty of having these 'things' in our lives today.

Please do not lose focus on today. I know through painful experience that constantly looking at tomorrow leaves you very discontented with what you have around and with you now. Keep an eye on the future but totally enjoy everything you do and have at this moment.

Who am I now? I believe I have matured and grown up as a man. Sounds crazy at 48, but I now know that through my journey from childhood to adulthood there were great gaps of self reliance that I had had no opportunity to place within my portfolio of skills or experiences.

The massive trauma I experienced was a really hard lesson, leaving me with absolutely no option but to look specific parts of me in the face, in reality, for the first time. Through the journey I have travelled, I know that I will never again have a perception that I cannot survive on my own. I know I can support myself not only financially but, of much more significance, I can support myself emotionally.

I can now see all of the pieces that have been added to my life through this experience. I have an understanding of the beauty of friendships that I previously only perceived other people had. I have a brilliant network of truly close friends, ones where we share each others' challenges, delights, struggles and laughter.

I have developed a social life that I once only yearned for, but now I have it. I can now dance and truly enjoy the emotions and energy that cascade from people when they are truly in the moment. I react spontaneously to situations and opportunities that reveal themselves to me during the course of the day. My weeks seem to fill somehow with activities that beforehand I would be pushing to find, but just allowing them to flow to me is so much easier. That saying 'easy is right' has never been more profound.

I now have a relationship with my parents that had been missing for many years. The bond has grown stronger, yes, initially from necessity on my part, but now I have also allowed myself to see the real wisdom and beauty that they have within them, and I love and respect them fully now for who they are, and not perhaps for what I wanted them to be.

So who am I now? I believe the biggest gift I have given myself is permission to move on. By truly taking the time to look at where I was in my life I had the opportunity to see where things had gone wrong, where the mistakes had been made, and I determined to put my own things right. A massive lesson I have learnt is that the only person you can change is yourself. You may wish for your partner to change so that you can still be together, to overcome the issues that exist and I spent huge amounts of energy on this with my wife, especially during the last 5 or 6 years of our relationship. But how did she interpret my desire to change things? She thought I was nagging, I was criticising, I was pushing, I was difficult. Nothing I ever did was a deliberate attempt to hurt my wife; I just wanted us to change so we could go forward as a couple.

So who am I now? I think that I am a really nice guy. I am caring, good humoured, giving and, I hope, real. I now know that for so much of my life I had been working through a belief system, coupled with limiting fears, that caused me to continually send myself the message that I did not like myself.

This self criticism created the conditions where I could not truly love others. I could not be fully open, I could not be really there with other people because I had this little devil in my head saying that I was not good enough, that I needed to do more, that I needed to prove more. I had a belief that only when I had done all of 'those things' could I realise what

I so wanted. It was always tomorrow, just not today. Well, no more. I now feel that I am a great person. A very un-British statement, but if I don't think I am great who else will?

Another crucial lesson I have learnt from this experience is that if I continued doing what I had always done before I would get the same result again. I could not let that happen. I wanted to ensure that I did not take any 'baggage' into my next relationship, for the sake of my, and our, future happiness.

I can now make some tough decisions that are right for my life, and not continually put other's needs before mine. This, for me, has been a deeply challenging area as the thought of making decisions that are right for me appears selfish and possibly upsetting for the other person. I am not advocating selfishness here taken to a mercenary position. For me a relationship is about everyone involved, but that also includes me.

Strange as it may seem, I am now convinced that if you ensure that the decisions you take are right for you then they will be the right ones for the other party too. They might not see it at that point in time, but it was certainly the case for me when my wife said she "no longer loved me the way she had before".

Exercise 24 - Who Are You Now?

- *Who are you now?*
- *What have you determined you will and won't allow in your life?*
- *How have you evolved as a person through this journey?*
- *What negative thoughts are you still holding onto that are stopping you moving forward?*

- *How has your decision making process changed, are you using your feelings and emotions to guide you, allied to your thoughts and processes?*
- *How do you now feel about yourself, and what do you have to offer another? Remember, we are talking here about you, not the external but the internal, all of the aspects that make 'you' you.*
- *Are you now ready for your next relationship?*

A complete review of the realisations, changes and conclusions reached during this re-programming of your thoughts and attitudes. Please remember, deep change takes time, resilience and patience. The much used saying 'the journey of 1000 miles starts with the first step' has never been more pertinent. You are changing habits and beliefs held for many years but with diligent practise you will transform your future relationship life.

Join the Hope Club

When things seem dark, when every door that you open appears to have a brick wall behind it, when you face another disappointment, sometimes the only thing left is to hope things will change. A dream with faith, belief, perseverance and hope are all the ingredients you need to achieve anything you wish. However, the revealing of your dreams will not always be in accord with your delivery time demands.

Journal Entry - 18th December

I didn't want to write in the journal yesterday or today. I met someone at dancing last night. It was one of those moments. I saw her and then there was no other woman in the room. She is in my view stunning, very slim and when I spoke to her she has a heart that is broken and like mine in need of repair.

A major difference with her is her positioning. She is a teacher, loves to be a free spirit and is fairly gregarious. Last night I gave her my number as she did not want to give hers. Today at 12 I got a text saying she was not worried – a reference to my note to her with my number on it that said "I am a good guy, don't worry" – she said she was intrigued; this is the first time anyone has called me this! I called her at 7.45pm but she said it was not a good time to talk but she was free all day tomorrow.

This situation feels very different. It is the first time I have experienced the thoughts that I may not be educated enough, I may not have enough depth, I may not yet be strong enough. You know what? I am going to be me and if this is not good enough then it is not meant to be.

I really believe this is a response from all of my thoughts and dreams. I have changed trying to work things out and am leaving it to happen, not forcing. I do sometimes drift but I am now aware and drag myself back on track.

I have not told anyone about this meeting, not even Gary. This is because I do not want to break any spell that might be involved. I feel that I really have to take this in small stages. She is the first woman since the happening who has made me feel really different inside and I want to let it mature at its own pace.

She is stunning. I feel there is depth untapped. I can't say at this stage that I am smitten but I really want to experience this relationship to see where it can go.

I know you are going to say to yourself, "He's ok, he got himself sorted really quickly, job done, perfect world, happily ever after, just follow the steps in his bloody book, and bingo!" I am sorry to disappoint you. Although this relationship did flourish into a massive attraction and a deep love, for a variety of reasons we are no longer together.

I do not want to go heavily into this next phase of my life other than to say that the chance to meet someone else was truly amazing. The opportunity to feel totally captivated by someone in all dimensions was beautiful and demonstrated to me that there was indeed life after the event. Not just an existence, not just getting through the day, not just a battle to put your shoes on in the morning, but a vibrant life with energy, passion, lightness and purpose.

I had spent the previous 5 months coming to terms with a life shift so dramatic for me that I had really no idea who I was

179

anymore. My saving grace had been my ability to keep myself going through the formulation of my dream. My dream gave me a purpose, it gave me hope. It gave me positive feelings and pictures to offset all of the negative thoughts running through my mind. My dream literally allowed me to 'dream' at those times when darkness appeared all around.

Within my dream I built a new life where once again I had a loving family surrounding me. I could feel the buzz of energy through the walls doors and windows of our new house with people talking, laughing and caring. I could see how the rooms would be decorated, how the kitchen layout allowed air into the home, how the house opened up to back onto fields with an area greatly enjoyed by my faithful hound. I had rebuilt my finances to enable me to thoroughly enjoy my new life. I was able to support my son and my parents whilst building a legacy for the future. I still worked hard doing what I loved to do whilst being well rewarded for helping others. I had a fantastic range of friends with whom we enjoyed meals, fun and great conversation. To top it all, I had alongside me the most fantastic woman who I adored and we were completely devoted to one another. Perfect.

My dream has remained consistent since the day it was written. This consistency is not through inflexibility (I hope!) it is due to the fact that all of the components of the dream feel instinctively 'right' to and for me. I am totally clear on what I want in my life. The creation of my dream has been a complete revelation to me.

Within my dream, where are the fast cars, exotic holidays, Rolex watches, 100 notches on my bedpost, a mansion, a swimming pool, a private jet? You could say I have low aspirations. I would respond, having had this fantastic opportunity to re-evaluate my whole life, that I now know what is fundamentally important to me. I have discovered that whilst these additional items listed would indeed be nice to have, I don't need them. I don't need them to allow me to feel totally happy and contented.

So, after meeting this lady dancing, resulting in another 'failed' relationship, have all of my dreams been shattered? Have I deluded myself, have I set myself up for an almighty fall? I would contend that this relationship happened to prepare me for what is coming in my life. On reflection, I can now see what this relationship gave me and for these things I will forever be grateful. It rebuilt my faith in myself, allowed me to share what I am with another and proved that, given time, life starts to reappear as never before.

Have all of the elements of my dream come true now? Far from it, but I know that they will. Ask me how I know? I just do. I know through having belief that they will reveal themselves when the time is right. I now realise that these experiences are all parts of my journey and you cannot force your plans into reality against their due time. You have to let these things develop at their own pace, at their own speed. Your dream is not on the same clock as you. This is fundamental to understand. Don't be disheartened because it does not happen quickly. If it is right for you, and you truly believe in and have faith in what you want, it will come to you at the right time, I assure you.

Throughout this book I have encouraged you to strip away all of the masks you have been wearing for many years. You have been asked to think deeply about what is important in your life. You have been pushed to look at yourself and re-discover who you were before the journey you have travelled took its toll. You have been requested to create a new future based upon a dream. Now, I am challenging you to truly believe in what you have written for your future life.

Your dream is designed to give you hope that there are better things just around the corner. The word hope is a very 'floppy' word, a word overused, a word that says something and nothing all at once. However, consider for a moment a world where there is no hope. Can you think of a more desperate place to be found?

Let's start now to enjoy what we have in our life today. Let's start having fun with a belief that we have truly moved forward in finding ourselves again. Life wants us to be happy. Allow life to happen and, combined with your own efforts, all that you desire will be revealed.

The dictionary describes hope as 'to expect, to trust, to anticipate, to wish, to look forward to'. Hope is a magnificent word; believe in it!

Practice Definitions

Neuro-linguistic programming (NLP) is defined in 3 ways. It is a model of interpersonal communication chiefly concerned with the relationship between successful patterns of behaviour and the subjective experiences (especially patterns of thought) that underlay them. It is a system of alternative therapy which seeks to educate people in self-awareness and effective communication. It enables change of unhelpful patterns of mental and emotional behaviour. The co-founders, Richard Bandler and linguist John Grinder, claimed it would be instrumental in "finding ways to help people have better, fuller and richer lives". They created the title to denote a connection between neurological processes ('neuro'), language ('linguistic') and behavioural patterns that have been learned through experience ('programming') which can be organised to achieve specific goals in life.

NLP was originally promoted by its founders, Bandler and Grinder, in the 1970s as an extraordinarily effective and rapid form of psychological therapy, capable of addressing the full range of problems which psychologists are likely to encounter, such as phobias, depression, habit disorder, psychosomatic illnesses, learning disorders. It also espoused the potential for self-determination through overcoming learned limitations and emphasized well-being and healthy functioning. Later, it was promoted as a 'science of excellence', derived from the study or 'modelling' of how successful or outstanding people in different fields obtain their results. These skills can be learned by anyone to improve their effectiveness both personally and professionally.

Buddhism is a family of beliefs and practises variously described as religious, spiritual and philosophical. These are all based on the teachings of Siddhartha Gautama, commonly known as the Buddha, (Sanskrit for "awakened one")

Born in what is today Nepal, the Buddha lived and taught in the north eastern region of the Indian subcontinent. Adherents recognize the Buddha as an awakened teacher who shared his insights with people to allow them to escape the cycle of suffering and rebirth. The Buddha's teachings provide instructions on how to understand the true nature of phenomena, end suffering, and achieve nirvana.

Buddhism, as traditionally conceived, is a path of salvation. Buddhists use various methods to liberate themselves and others from the suffering of worldly existence. These include: ethical conduct and altruism; devotional practices; ceremonies; the invocation of bodhisattvas; renunciation; meditation; the cultivation of mindfulness and wisdom; and physical exercises.

Modern Psychology is an academic and applied discipline involving the systematic, and often scientific, study of human/animal mental functions and behaviour. Occasionally, in addition or opposition to employing the scientific method, it also relies on symbolic interpretation and critical analysis, although it often does so less prominently than other social sciences such as sociology. Psychologists study such phenomena as perception, cognition, attention, emotion, motivation, personality, behaviour and interpersonal relationships. Some, especially depth psychologists, also study the unconscious mind.

Psychological knowledge is applied to various spheres of human activity, including issues related to everyday life—such as family, education and employment—and to the treatment of mental health problems. Psychologists attempt to understand the role of mental functions in individual and social behaviour, while also exploring the underlying physiological and neurological processes. Psychology includes many sub-fields of study and applications concerned with such areas as human development, sports, health, industry, media and law. Psychology incorporates research from the natural sciences, social sciences and humanities.

Transactional analysis, commonly known as **TA**, is an integrative approach to the theory of psychology and psychotherapy. It is integrative because it has elements of psychoanalytic, humanist and cognitive approaches. It was developed by Canadian-born US psychiatrist Eric Berne during the late 1950s.

TA is a theory of personality and a systematic psychotherapy for personal growth and personal change.

As a theory of personality, TA describes how people are structured psychologically. It uses what is perhaps its best known model, the ego-state (Parent-Adult-Child) model to do this. This same model helps us to understand how people function and express themselves in their behaviours.

As a theory of communication it extends to a method of analysing systems and organisations. It introduces the idea of a "Life (or Childhood) Script", that is, a story one perceives about one's own life, to answer questions such as *"What matters"*, *"How do I get along in life"* and *"What kind of person am I"*. This story, TA says, is often stuck to no matter the consequences, to "prove" one is right, even at the cost of pain, compulsion, self-defeating behaviour and other dysfunction. Thus TA offers a theory of a broad range of psychopathology.

In practical application, it can be used in the diagnosis and treatment of many types of psychological disorders, and provides a method of therapy for individuals, couples, families and groups.

Outside the therapeutic field, it has been used in education, to help teachers remain in clear communication at an appropriate level, in counselling and consultancy, in management and communications training, and by other bodies.

Quantum physics is a branch of science that deals with discrete, indivisible units of energy called quanta as described by the Quantum Theory. There are five main ideas represented in Quantum Theory:

1. Energy is not continuous, but comes in small but discrete units
2. The elementary particles behave both like particles *and* like waves.
3. The movement of these particles is inherently random.
4. It is *physically impossible* to know both the position and the momentum of a particle at the same time. The more precisely one is known, the less precise the measurement of the other is.
5. The atomic world is *nothing* like the world we live in.

While at a glance this may seem like just another strange theory, it contains many clues to the fundamental nature of the universe. Furthermore, it describes the nature of the universe as being fundamentally different to the world we see. As Niels Bohr said, "Anyone who is not shocked by quantum theory has not understood it."

Aligned to our personal and emotional health, a principle statement of quantum physics insists that 'thoughts are things'. Therefore, the quality of our thoughts, be they positive or negative in nature, empowering or constricting, create the circumstances we constantly experience. Hence, thoughts are causes that create effects or outcomes.

Physicists have discovered that quantum 'particles' make decisions. These particles are powered by intelligence. The acceptance that each individual is connected on an unseen level enables this intelligent thought to bring about the manifestation of the desired, or undesired, result.

A definition that accompanies quantum physics, at this level of explanation, reveals "you get what you think about on a consistent basis, whether you want it or not"

Cognitive Behaviour Therapy, CBT is a psychotherapeutic approach that aims to influence dysfunctional emotions, behaviours and cognitions through a goal oriented, systematic procedure. CBT can be seen as an umbrella term for a number of psychological techniques that share a theoretical basis in behaviouristic learning and cognitive psychology.

CBT is effective for the treatment of a variety of problems, including mood, anxiety, personality, eating, substance abuse, and psychotic disorders. Treatment is often brief, and time-limited. CBT is used in individual therapy as well as group settings, and the techniques are often adapted for self-help applications.

CBT was primarily developed through a merging of behaviour therapy with cognitive therapy. While rooted in rather different theories, these two traditions found common ground in focussing on the 'here and now' and on alleviating symptoms. CBT is the treatment of choice for a number of mental health difficulties, including post-traumatic stress disorder, OCD, bulimia nervosa and clinical depression.